I0843297

The Cactus and other Tropical Succulents

Aloes, Agaves, Sempervivums, Sedums, Mesembranthemums and others

by Henry Allnutt

with an introduction by Roger Chambers

This work contains material that was originally published in 1877.

*This publication was created and published for the public benefit,
utilizing public funding and is within the Public Domain.*

*This edition is reprinted for educational purposes
and in accordance with all applicable Federal Laws.*

Introduction Copyright 2018 by Roger Chambers

Self Reliance Books

Get more historic titles on animal and stock breeding, gardening and old fashioned skills by visiting us at:

http://selfreliancebooks.blogspot.com/

Introduction

I am pleased to present yet another title on Ginseng.

The work is in the Public Domain and is re-printed here in accordance with Federal Laws.

As with all reprinted books of this age that are intended to perfectly reproduce the original edition, considerable pains and effort had to be undertaken to correct fading and sometimes outright damage to existing proofs of this title. At times, this task is quite monumental, requiring an almost total "rebuilding" of some pages from digital proofs of multiple copies. Despite this, imperfections still sometimes exist in the final proof and may detract from the visual appearance of the text.

I hope you enjoy reading this book as much as I enjoyed making it available to readers again.

Roger Chambers

PREFACE.

We publish this small work respecting the Cactus and other Succulents without any attempt to write a botanical treatise on the subject. This remark, however, applies only to our own observations. The extracts we give from several standard books and from living authorities convey, without doubt, valuable information. As we have experienced a growing interest in these curious plants, we are fain to believe that others will derive much pleasure in their leisure moments if they do as we have done; and we shall endeavour in the following pages to convey to them the knowledge we have acquired, limited as that may be.

Speaking of Succulents, Mr. Shirley Hibberd says, "The capability of bearing any amount of sun-light renders these plants admirably adapted for the possessors of those little glass boxes which in town houses are called conservatories; for, unfit as these structures usually are for plants growing, they answer well for sheltering succulents and hard leaved plants of small size on account of their dryness and strong light. The wonderful variety, both in form and colour, that may be ensured in a collection of these plants costing almost nothing in the first instance, and the very small space occupied by them, if judiciouly selected, are additional reasons in favour of their adoption by amateurs, who value a little bit of glass more highly than to waste it on ephemeral plants that can only be properly grown in comparatively large and well-appointed plant houses."

Beautiful as Camellias are when in flower, those who keep them in small conservatories must be content to remain for months without a blossom; in fact, as you walk into most of such places they appear to contain only an assemblage of dark green shrubs, very uninteresting to our mind; and even if there are a few other plants, it requires but a momentary glance to take them all in. We know them at once, and we walk out just as a person does on retiring from a room without a picture or anything to attract his special attention. Not so with succulents; of these there is such a vast variety of plants that, as respects the description here given of three or four score, we do but touch the hem of the garment.

In the Royal Gardens at Kew, and in Mr. J. T. Peacock's admirable collection at Sudbury House, Hammersmith, and at the Alexandra Palace, we see an astonishing variety of succulents. Mr. J. R. Jackson, Curator of the Museums at Kew, in page 20, tells us that there are 950 species of Cacti, and these do not include Aloes, Agaves, Echeverias, Euphorbias, Gasterias, Mesembryanthemums, Sedums, Sempervivums,—their names is indeed legion.

We wish to impress on the minds of our readers two important facts. First, these plants take up very little room; where you have five or six Fuchsias or Geraniums there is ample space for a dozen or twenty Cacti; and, secondly, the form of most succulents is so remarkable that they are always worthy of close examination whether they are in flower or not. We mean that the interest we may feel in a Cactus does not depend solely on its flowering, as is the case with the generality of plants.

Our readers should remember that our object in writing this work is to supply information to those who, like ourselves, have no conservatory, and who therefore can but have a small collection of these plants.

Should any one possess greater facilities than we enjoy, supposing they are not satisfied with what contents us, there is ample scope to soar higher than we go. He can, if he has a hot-house, commence regularly with one genus, as Mr. Croucher recommends in his practical directions to amateurs, which will be found in our pages; and, after mastering this, proceed onwards; or, if he pleases, he can turn his attention to grafting one plant on another, or producing hybrids. There is no lack of novelty here. Mr. Shirley Hibberd speaks of his collection of one hundred and twenty-five species of Mesembryanthemums. Surely there is field enough for the most energetic of aspiring gardeners.

Need we say more to introduce our subject.

CONTENTS.

PLATES.

CACTI IN PLATE 1.

(See Frontispiece.)

1. Echinopsis formosa.
2. Mammillaria pusilla.
3. Echinopsis vallida.
4. Echinocactus Pfersdorffii.
5. Mammillaria conopsea.
6. Echinocactus cornigerus.
7. Mammillaria Fisherii.
8. Melocactus communis— Turk's Cap.
9. Pilocereus Williamsi.
10. Pilocerus semilis—Old Man Cactus.
11. Pilocereus fossulatus.
12. Mammillaria nivea.
13. Echinocactus ornatus.
14. Mammillaria crucigera.
15. Mammilaria acanthophlegma.
16. Cereus chilensis.
17. Mammillaria polygona.
18. Mammillaria Parkinsoni.
19. Mammillaria elephantidens.
20. Echinocactus helophorus.
21. Echinocactus myriostigma.
22. Mammillaria densa.
23. Echinocactus Pfiefferi.
24. Mammillaria phymatothele.
25. Echinocactus odierii.
26. Mammillaria dolichocentra.
27. Echinopsis formosa.
28. Mammillaria semperiræ.

PLANTS RUNNING UP THE WINDOWS.

Above No. 8. Hoya australis.
" " 21. Stauntonia latifolia.

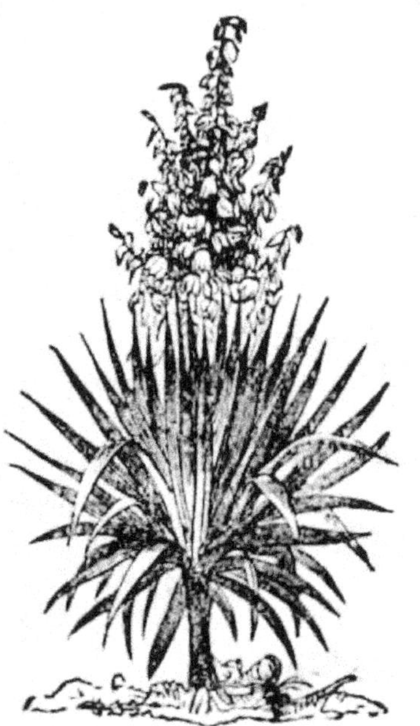

Fig. 58.—YUCCA GLORIOSA.

We have one of these noble plants in our garden.

THE CACTUS

AND OTHER

SUCCULENTS.

"O Lord, how manifold are Thy works! in wisdom hast Thou made them all."—Ps. civ. 24.

Lord Chancellor Bacon remarks that gardening is the purest of human pleasures. Without doubt, this is true; but, unfortunately, there are about five months out of the twelve in which little or nothing can be done in a flower garden. From the middle of October to the middle or end of March pleasurable gardening may be said to be in abeyance. You may have a few bulbs, but these are expensive. Their flowers last but a brief time; Crocuses, especially, fall down and wither almost as soon as they bloom, it is also especially annoying to find that sparrows eat them when they begin to flower; this, at least, is our experience, and even allowing that you have a good show of Hyacinths and other bulbs, the weather is such that you cannot be out frequently in the garden to see them.

The only way in which a person can enjoy the hobby of gardening throughout the year is by having a Conservatory; but this is beyond the means of most men of the middle class. And when a greenhouse is possessed, it entails considerable trouble and expense to fill it with suitable plants and attending to the temperature; for one night's frost may ruin valuable plants. Therefore, with the view of filling up this void in the year, we have lately turned our attention to plants of the *Cactus* family, and exceedingly interesting we find them. These curious succulents belong exclusively to the new world, as the Heaths to the old.

The name *Cactus* was first used by Theophrastus to denote a spiny plant of Sicily, but this is considered doubtful; at all events, the *Cacti* of Central America must have been unknown at that period.

The *Cactus* family is composed of several hundred species of tropical succulents, almost always unprovided with leaves, and of the most varied and grotesque form. The absence of leaves is compensated by the enduring moisture of the outer skin of the stem which is coloured green, and is capable of performing the functions of ordinary leaves. From its thickness and impervious texture, the undue evaporation from the tissues underneath, to which it would be otherwise subject in hot climates, is prevented. The spines are rudimentary leaves.

Humboldt says there is hardly anything in vegetable physiognomy which makes so singular and ineffaceable an impression on a newly-arrived traveller as the sight of an arid plain thickly covered like those of Cumana, New Barcelona, and Coro, in the province of Jaen de Bracamosos, with columnar and candelabra-like divided *Cactus* stems. Dr. Engleman also remarks, that as far as the eye can reach in the valleys or on the mountains of Mexico, little else but rocky boulders and the stately yet awfully sombre aspect of the *Cereus giganteus* can be seen. These latter attain a height of forty or fifty feet in the table land of South California.

A drawing is given of these wonderful plants, or *Cereus* trees, in an American work treating of the boundary between Mexico and the United States. They stand up in the most gaunt, formal manner, and would give one the idea of telegraph posts or the poles of a gymnasium—not a leaf to be seen. Some send forth branches from the stem, which grow at first almost at right angles, but afterwards start upwards parallel with the stem, and maintain nearly the same thickness throughout, like enormous gas standards.

This work remarks that the juice of the *Cactus* serves as a substitute for water when it cannot otherwise be procured. Instances have been known amongst the white trappers in Mexico where the lives of men have been saved by them—also that one species of the *Opuntia* is armed with spines worse than those of the porcupine, and are the horror of man and beast—the barbed spines stick so fast in the flesh that the joint of the plant is separated from the main stem before the spine can be withdrawn. The

O. Tuna form hedges fifteen to twenty feet high. A shrubby species of the *Opuntia frutescens* is abundant all over the southern part of Mexico and Texas, and is very ornamental, specially when loaded with its scarlet berries.

Fig. 2.

SCENE IN CENTRAL AMERICA—THE CEREUS, OPUNTIA AND CACTUS.

Speaking of Honduras,* Mr. Squier says:—"On some of the plains, as on that of Comayagua (the capital of that country), the varying forms of *Cacti* become distinguishing features, frequently attaining to gigantic size, and almost taking the character of

---

* From "Pictures of Travel in Far-off Lands." Published by Nelson & Sons, Paternoster-row, and Edinburgh.

forests. Here they stud the ground, spherical and spinated, warning man and beast against incautious tread ; yet radiating from their grooved sides flowers and fruits of delicate ruby, in shape and colour like glasses of tenderest crystal, flowing over with ruddy wine of golden Burgundy. There they rise in tall, fluted columns, appearing in the exaggerating twilight like the ruins of ancient temples. And still beyond we see them, articulated and jointed, spreading their broad succulent palms, silvered with the silky habiliments of the scarlet cochineal. And yet again, lavish of contrasting forms, they trail like serpents over the ground, and twine themselves in knotty coils around fallen trunks and among the crevices of the barren rocks. Here, too, the *Agave* appears, with its dense green clusters of spiny-edged leaves, shooting up its tall stem to flower but once, scatter forth its thousand bulbs, and then to die. . . . . Some varieties of *Cactus*, particularly that of which the long-tangled arms are prismatic in form, do not disdain to fix themselves in the forks of the Calabash-tree, and overwhelm it with their own more rapid growth."

The *Cactus* family live to such an age that we find them employed, not only as hedges between land, but also to denote national boundaries; such, for instance, as between the English and French possessions in the island of St. Christopher, in the West Indies. Mere trees would be unfitted for such a purpose, for they might be cut down for their timber, or, in course of time, fall from natural decay; whereas the *Cactus* may be said to be imperishable in the West Indies. Some writers call them vegetable statues, and well they may, for it is not possible to estimate their age; they differ little in appearance during a period of twenty-five years, and, indeed, stand for centuries. The flowers they yield are extremely large for the size of the plant, and are most beautiful. The fruit they bear is of a pleasant acid flavour, very refreshing in the tropics, both to men and animals.

"Wanderer," when writing in the *Gardener's Magazine*, and comparing England with the homes of the *Cactus*, says in his vigorous language :—" It is true that there is more real beauty in the outskirts of an English hamlet where the great oaks give shade to fat cattle and sheep than in the dusty sunburnt plains, the unshaded rocky acclivities, and the vast rolling desert of sand and nitrous efflorescence, where many of these strange *Cactus* plants bask in the sun like basilisks, and seem almost as weird and ominous in their gauntness, their hardness, their forbidding complexion, and their impassiveness. The last-named is perhaps the most provoking of all their attributes. A respectable plant, such as for example a geranium or a cabbage, would shrivel up and drop dead and pass out of visibility as mere dust in some of the ever-roasted regions where the fleshy cactuses live on unhurt and unmoved, so horribly impassive that it exasperates the traveller who is sickening amid the monotony of roasted sierras to see that the plants that dot the dreary waste make no sign of a change, and evidently care for nothing but a burning blaze of sunshine and a handful of sand. The wild horses may kick the cactuses to pieces to get a little of their tasteless juice to prevent death by thirst, and what do the cactuses that have been kicked care about it? Nothing! They remain unmoved until the rainy season returns, by which time their wounds have been healed by the burning sun, and they make a bound into new growth with such vigour that even Frankenstein is a fool to it."

The bloom of the *Cactus* is white, orange, red, and yellow; even it is said that blue is not altogether wanting, for the azure tints which largely ornament the inner petals of some of this family of plants is well known.

The *Cactus* occupies a large geographical area; from the centre of America they advance northwards as far as the fiftieth degree of latitude, and extend to the same degree south, a distance of 7,000 miles.

They are to be observed on the coast, the plains, and the mountains that border the Atlantic and Pacific oceans, and some are found in the Andes and Cordillera mountains nearly as high as the eternal snow. They abound in Mexico, also in Brazil; but in this latter country they diminish in size. Some are hairy, to preserve them from the cold, and are so large that, at a distance, they appear like a flock of sheep. One species of the *Cactus* is reported to be the principal food for the land tortoises in the Gallopagus.

We believe our readers will feel interested if extracts are given from several standard works on gardening in which succulents are treated. It appears that there is no book in the English language devoted exclusively to these plants, excepting a curious old work written and published by Richard Bradley, from the "Lamb," beyond Temple Bar, in 1716.* We cannot but sympathise with him when he remarks in the preface to his treatise, that "he designed having fifty figures of succulent plants in the book; but, finding that the *spirit of Botany was not powerful enough* to pay the expense of engraving the copper-plates, he was obliged to discontinue his thoughts of publishing the work, till now, at the desire of some friends, he renewed his former resolution of printing it." Mr. Bradley proposed to issue the work in ten numbers, but he stops at the fifth, which we have had the pleasure of looking over at the British Museum. He only gives plates and descriptions of five *Cacti*, viz., the *Great Upright Torch Thistle;* the "*Small Six Rib'd,*" as he writes it; the *Three Rib'd;* the *Pinpillow,* or *Minion*

---

* It is a singular coincidence that our office is almost opposite the spot where the "Lamb" formerly stood. That house, with two others, was taken for the erection of Messrs. Gosling's Bank in 1767. Thus, after a lapse of about 160 years, we take up the thread of Mr. Bradley's discourse.

Prickly Pear (evidently an *Opuntia*); and, fifthly, the *White Torch Thistle*. The book contains several plates of the *Stapelia* (see page 110) and the *Fig-Marigold*, another name for the *Mesembryanthemum*; also the *Small Pearled Aloe*—we think he means the *Haworthia attenuata* (see page 96). Mr. Bradley says that the *Torch Thistle* (*Cactus*) was first raised in England at the Bishop of London's Palace, Fulham, and that it flowered in July or August. He further remarks that two *Aloes* at Hampton Court flowered in 1714. The stems of each were seventeen feet high, and had no less than five flower stems on each, which continued to bloom for twelve months, and then both " dy'd." This curious old book is written in Latin on one side and English on the other, and each part had a title page in the two languages, and cost 2s.—a great sum in those days.

We now proceed to give a lengthy extract from Loudon's excellent " Encyclopædia of Plants." He says the *Cacti* family consist of succulents (juicy, moist plants) of perennial duration, generally without leaves (there are some exceptions), and having the stems or branches jointed. They are for the most part armed with spines in bundles. These bundles of spines are placed on the top of the tubercles on the smaller *Melon Cactus*, which is tubercled all over, and produces its flowers between the tubercles. In the great *Melon Cactus* the spines are arranged in a single row on the ridge of the ribs. These are of an ovate or globular form. Those on the *Torch-*

Cactus, on the contrary, are slender, rise up high, and are jointed and branched. Many of them are almost cylindrical, with from five to ten shallow ribs; some, however, are square or three-cornered. The structure of the *Creeping Cereus* (a name signifying pliant, like wax, as the shoots are easily bent) is the same with these, except that the stems are weak and cannot support themselves. They, therefore, seek support from trees, and throw out roots from the stem, like ivy.

Fig. 3.   Fig. 4.

OPUNTIA FICUS-INDICA   PHYLLOCACTUS ACKERMANNI.
(INDIAN FIG).

In the *Indian Fig* the branches are jointed and flattened like the sole of a shoe. The bundles of spines are scattered over the surface, and the flowers are produced from the edge of the extreme branches.

In the *Phyllocactus* the branches are thinner; they are indented along the edge, and the flowers come out singly from the indentures. This seldom has any spines. *Pereskia*, the *Cactus* alluded to with leaves, has a round stalk with leafy branches; the leaves alternate, flat and thick; the prickles are large and stiff, and come out in bundles on the stalk and branches, chiefly at the axils (literally the arm-pits, viz., the point of union of the leaf and stem); the flowers are produced, several together, from the axils also. In this and the *Indian Fig* the flowers are pitcher-shaped. In the other species they are sub-cylindrical and longer; in the *Phyllocactus* very long. The fruit in some of the sorts is small, like currants; but in others it is larger and shaped like a fig, whence their name of *Indian Fig*.

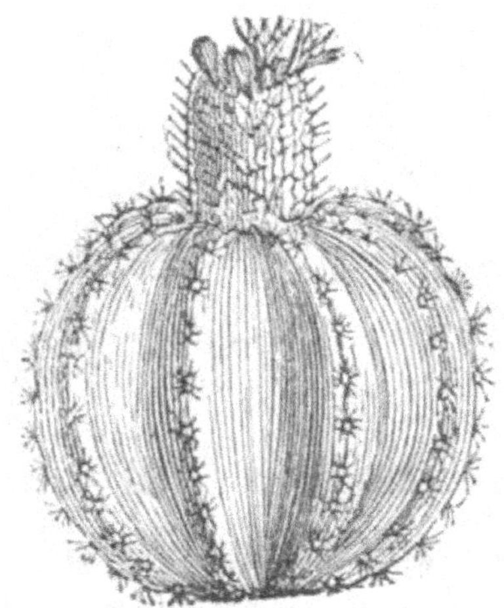

Fig. 5.—MELOCACTUS COMMUNIS (TURK'S CAP).

The *Turk's Cap Cactus* (*Melocactus communis*) appears like a large melon, with deep ribs, the elevations set all over with knots of strong, sharp thorns. When divided through the middle the inside is found to be a soft, green, fleshy substance, very full of moisture. The flowers and fruit are produced in circles round the upper part of the cap. Some of those brought to England have been more than a yard in circumference and two and a-half feet high, including the cap; but in the West Indies these *Cacti* are nearly twice this size. Linnæus remarks that this plant resembles a hedgehog (we should say rather the sea-urchin) in its form and species; the top has a convex, shaggy body, with long loose hair, from which the flowers proceed.

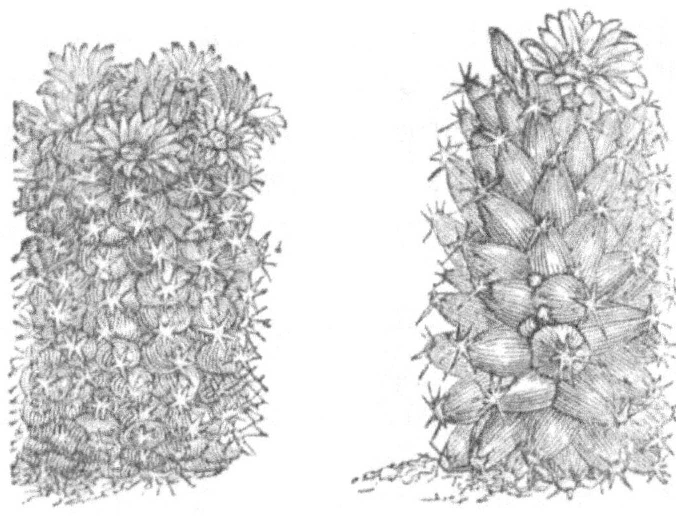

Fig. 6. *Fig.* 7.

MAMMILLARIA LEHMANNI. MAMMILLARIA ATRATA.

The *Melocactus, Mammillaria,* and *Pilocereus* grow upon the steep, rocky mountain sides in the hottest part of America, where they seem to be thrust out of the apertures, having apparently little or no earth to support them; their roots shooting down into the fissures of the rocks a considerable depth, so that it is troublesome to get the plants up. In times of great drought, the cattle repair to the barren rocks where these *Cacti* grow, rip them up with their horns, tear off the outside skin, and greedily devour all the fleshy moist part. The fruit is freqently eaten by the inhabitants of the West Indies. It is about three-quarters of an inch long, of a taper form, drawing to a point at the bottom, but blunt at the top. The taste is an agreeable acid.

Cereus repandus, or wavy-angled, has a fruit about the size and shape of a Bergamot pear, having many soft spines on the skin. The outside is pale yellow, the inside very white, full of pulp having a great number of small black seeds lodged in it. It frequently flowers in July, and in warm seasons will perfect its fruit, which has very little flavour in this country, but is frequently served up at table in the West India Islands.

Fig. 8.

CEREUS GRANDIFLORUS.

Fig. 9.

CEREUS FLAGELLIFORMIS.

Cereus grandiflorus and *C. flagelliformis* have flowers remarkable for their beauty and sweetness. The former, when arrived to a sufficient strength, will produce many exceedingly large, beautiful, sweet-scented flowers, like most of this kind of very short duration, scarcely continuing six hours full blown;

nor do the flowers ever open again when once closed. They begin to open at seven or eight o'clock in the evening, are fully blown by eleven o'clock, and by three or four in the morning they fade and hang down quite decayed; but during their short continuance there is scarcely a flower of greater beauty, or that makes a more magnificent appearance. For the calyx of the flower, when open, is nearly a foot in diameter; the inside of which, being of a splendid yellow colour, appears like the rays of a bright star. The outside is of a dark brown; the petals, being of a pure white, add to the lustre; the vast number of recurved stamens surrounding the style in the centre of the flower make a fine appearance; add to all this the fine scent of the flower, which perfumes the air to a considerable distance. There is scarcely any plant which deserves a place in the hothouse so much as this, especially as it may be trained against the wall, where it will not take up any room. It usually flowers in July, and when the plants are large, many flowers will open the same night, and there will be a succession of them for several nights together. None are succeeded here by any appearance of fruit.

Cereus flagelliformis produces a greater number of flowers than the foregoing sort; they come out in May, and sometimes earlier when the season is warm. The petals are of a fine pink colour, both within and without; they are not so numerous, and the tube of the flower is longer than that of the other. These flowers keep open three or four days, provided the weather, or the place where the plants stand, be not too warm ; and during their continuance they look very beautiful. This sort has very slender trailing branches, which require a support ; they are not jointed, nor do they extend so far as the other sort. Fruit sometimes succeeds the flower, but seldom ripens. (See page 96.)

Fig. 10.　　　　Fig. 11.

CEREUS REPANDUS.　　　CEREUS TRIANGULARIS.

Cereus triangularis, the strawberry pear, bears the best-flavoured fruit of any of the sorts ; it is slightly acid, and at the same time sweet, pleasant, and cooling. In Martinique and other West Indian islands it is much esteemed.

The *Opuntia vulgaris*, of the country of the Opuntiani, whose chief town was Opus, in the vicinity of Phocis, though, like others, a native of America, is now found growing wild on the sides of the roads between Rome and Naples and other parts of Italy. Gerarde says it was brought to England from Virginia, and Collinson had it from Newfoundland. It was fruited in Scotland in a stove by Justice in 1750, and since that time by Braddick in the open air near London. It lived six or seven years, and endured one exceeding hard winter. The compost in which he grew the *Opuntia* was one-half carbonate of lime, for which lime-rubbish from old buildings will answer; the remaining half consisted of equal portions of London clay and peat earth, having the acid neutralised by barilla; these were intimately blended and sifted. One square yard was considered sufficient for one plant, which was placed in the middle of a small artificial hillock, raised about eighteen inches above the surface of the ground, which should be rendered perfectly dry, if necessary, by under draining. Neither the leaves, flowers, nor fruit should ever be suffered to touch the ground, but they should be constantly kept from the earth by placing stones or bricks under them in imitation of rock-work.

Opuntia Ficus-indica is common in Jamaica, and on it feed the wild sort of cochineal insect. The fruit is large, and of a deep purple colour.

Opuntia Tuna (an Arabic word for fig) is used as a hedge plant in Spain, South America, and the West Indies. When the island of St. Christopher was to be divided between the English and the French, three rows of the *Tuna* were planted by common consent between the boundaries. Sir J. E. Smith remarks that the stamens of the flower are very irritable, and that if a feather be drawn through them, in two or three seconds they begin to lie down gently on one side, and in a short time become recumbent at the bottom of the flower.

Fig. 12.
OPUNTIA TUNA.

Fig. 13.
OPUNTIA COCHINILLIFERA.

Opuntia cochinillifera is the species on which the cochineal insect feeds. Although they will live on other succulents, this is preferred as least annoying by its prickles. It produces edible fruit larger than that of the *Opuntia vulgaris*. A red flower grows on the top of the fruit ; this, when the fruit is ripe, falls down on the top, and covers it from the rain or dew. In a day or two the flower is scorched up by the heat of the sun ; the fruit opens wide, and the inside appears full of small red insects. A large linen cloth is then spread under, and the plant is shaken with large sticks to disturb the insects, so that they take wing to be gone, but keep hovering over the place till, by the heat, they fall down dead on the cloth, where the Indians allow them to remain two or three days until they are dry.

Mr. Stephens, in his "Travels in Central America,"* relates that in Guatemala (west of Honduras) he

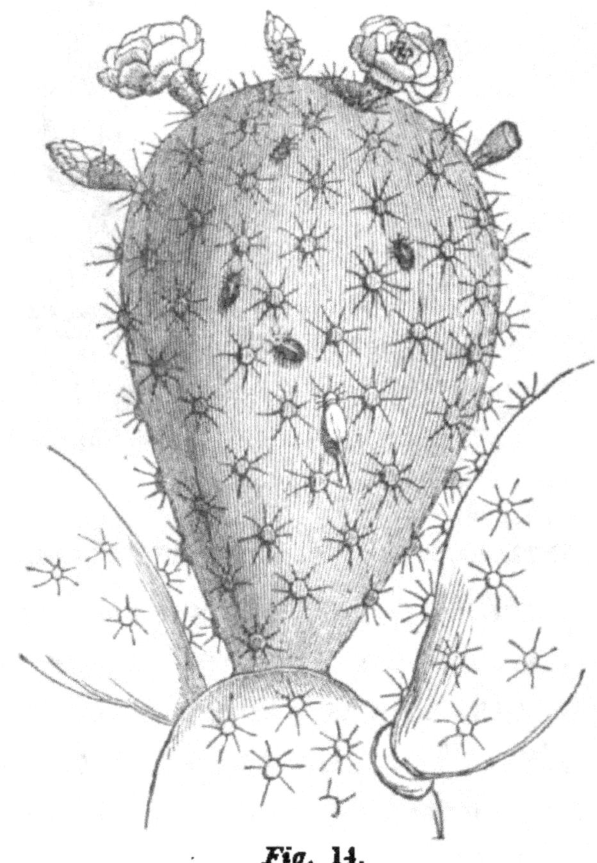

Fig. 14.

OPUNTIA COCHINILLIFERA WITH THE COCHINEAL INSECTS ON IT.

inspected the mode of the cultivation of the *Opuntia.* It was set out in rows like Indian corn, and was, at the time he visited the place, four feet high. On every leaf was pinned, with a thorn, a piece of cane,

---

* From " Pictures of Travel."   See note to page 4.

in the hollow of which were thirty or forty insects.
These insects cannot move, but breed, and the young
crawl out and fasten on the leaf. When they have
once fixed, they never move. A light film gathers
over them, and as they feed the leaves become
mildewed and white. At the end of the dry season
some of the leaves are cut off, and hung up in a
storehouse for seed ; the insects are brushed off from
the rest and dried, and are then sent abroad to
minister to the luxuries and elegancies of civilised
life, and enliven with their bright colours the
drawing-rooms of London and Paris. He said there
are about 70,000 insects in a pound. Mr. Stephens
adds : — "It seems strange that a creature much
resembling a bug in form, and not so large, should
be of so much importance to numbers of people ;
and that the vanity of others should be excited by
so small a cause as wearing robes dyed in this insect's
blood ! "

Fig. 15.—PERESKIA ACULEATA.

The genus *Pereskia* is named in memory of

N. F. Pieresk, of Aix. It has fruit the size of a walnut, having tufts of small leaves on it.

Sandy loam, or loam mixed with a little brick rubbish, is the best soil for all the *Cacti*. The pots should be as small as the plants will allow, and well drained. They require but little water.

We take the following from the pen of Mr. John R. Jackson, A.L.S., Curator of the Museums of Economic Botany, Kew, which appeared in the "Student" of April, 1870:—

"THE CACTUS FAMILY.

"The natural order *Cactaceæ* is a group of plants about which others than botanists, or even horticulturists, have some knowledge, for many of its members are well-known window plants, and the comparative rarity and beauty of their flowers cause them to be general favourites.

"The order numbers, according to the latest revision, thirteen genera and about 950 species. Their forms are variable: in some—*Cereus giganteus*, for instance—the stems grow to forty or fifty feet, and often columnar in form; in others they are huge masses of succulent matter, almost or quite spherical. The flowers are for the most part large and showy.

"In the genus *Cereus* some of the largest and most striking forms of the order occur, as well as the largest and most attractive flowers. The habits of the species vary considerably, some growing erect, others climbing up trees, while others trail along the ground. The forms of their trunks are also very variable, for while some are cylindrical, or perfectly columnar, others are angular, and others again are ribbed or furrowed.

" The most noble of all the species is the *Cereus giganteus*. This plant is we repeat forty or fifty feet high, and sometimes even to a height of sixty feet, with a diameter of two or more feet about half-way up, lessening somewhat towards the top and near the base. These plants are frequently unbranched throughout their entire height; some, however, send forth branches from their sides, which grow at first almost at right angles, but afterwards start upwards, parallel with the main trunk, and maintain nearly the same thickness throughout. The stems and branches are deeply furrowed or ribbed, the ribs being arranged at regular intervals from each other, from the base to the top. On the edge of these ribs, at distances of about an inch apart, are small tufts of a yellowish colour, bearing numerous short spines, amongst which are five or six longer ones. These plants are devoid of leaves, like most of the other *Cacti*, and begin to flower when about ten or twelve feet high. The flowers, which are of a light cream-colour, are composed of numerous petals and sepals, and measure some four or five inches long, and when fully expanded are of nearly equal diameter. They are borne in profusion on the summit of the stems and branches.

" *Cereus grandiflorus* is perhaps one of the best-known of these night-flowerers; it is a creeping plant, a native of the West Indies, scrambling over rocks or decayed trees; the branches are slightly angular, with five to seven angles. The flowers are very large when fully expanded, and cup-shaped. The sepals are of a deep yellow or yellowish orange colour, and the petals pure white; the stamens are long and numerous, tipped with linear oblong anthers of a bright yellow colour. The stigma is also yellow, composed of many rays diverging at right angles from the style. The flowers are very fragrant, opening late in the evening, and becoming fully expanded about ten or eleven o'clock. They last only one night, and droop very early in the morning. (See Fig. 8, page 13.)

"Another night-flowerer, *C. MacDonaldii*, though somewhat similar in the colour of the sepals, and identical in the pure white of the petals, produces larger flowers, which, when fully expanded, are quite fourteen inches in diameter. This species is a very free flowerer. Its habit is similar to that of *Cereus grandiflorus*, having creeping dark-green stems about the thickness of a man's finger, but slightly angular, with five blunt irregularly-placed angles. It grows very rapidly, throwing out its long, straggling branches in all directions. A fine plant exists at Kew, which flowers freely during the early summer months. The next plant, in point of magnificence, amongst the night-flowering series, is

C. triangularis. This species is so named from its triangular stems, which are, perhaps, slightly thicker than those of the last-named species ; but the plant has a similar creeping habit, and bears very large yellowish flowers. (See Fig. 11, page 15.)

" *Cereus Lemairei*, *C. pterogona*, *C. nycticalus*, and *C. rostratus* are all night-flowerers ; indeed, the whole of the true *Cerei* open in the evening, and most of them are closed by about eight o'clock in the morning. The temperature of the house in which they are grown, however, exercises a great influence on them : if the air is hot and dry the flowers last but eleven to fourteen hours, while in a cooler atmosphere they will last twenty hours.

" *Cereus Tweedii* is a small-growing plant, cylindrical in form, and furrowed or ribbed, bearing on the edges of the ribs numerous spines, four or five of which are longer and stouter than the rest. It flowers freely ; the flowers are of a rich orange-crimson colour, and these, when contrasted with the dark green of the stem, produce such a pleasing effect as to make the plant one of the prettiest of the family.

" *Cereus chilensis* is a native of Chili. It is an erect-growing plant, very evenly furrowed or ribbed, the ribs not sharply angled, as in many of the species, but the face of each one is rounded, and the spines set on with the greatest uniformity : the longest, thickest, and most prominent starts from near the centre of the mammillæ, pointing downwards; in a direct line with it is a shorter one pointing upwards; the spaces between these being filled on one side with five others alternately long and short, two, however, being longer than the other three; the length of the corresponding spines on either side being equal.

The most characteristic and striking in appearance is the *Old Man Cactus* (*Pilocereus senilis*), which attains a height of from twenty to thirty feet, with a diameter of nine to ten inches. It grows perfectly straight, is fluted or furrowed by narrow channels from the base to the very top. The ridges of the ribs are covered with tufts of spines placed very closely together, and surrounded with long white hairs; near the top these hairs are thicker and longer; indeed, they hang down to such a length as almost to hide the upper portion of the stem, and so give to the plant a really venerable and hoary aspect. It is owing to this appearance that the plant has received the common name of *Old Man Cactus,* as well as its specific name *senilis.*

" Many of the *Cacti* are noted for their tenacity of life, and the following instance is a good illustration of this peculiarity. A plant of *P. senilis,* which was growing in the *Cactus* house at Kew, and which actually got too high for the house, was removed to the new temperate house; the process of removing such a bulk of fleshy matter was, as might be expected, no easy task, especially when we consider the extreme sharpness of the multitudinous spines;

so the plant got slightly fractured across its trunk within eighteen inches or two feet of the top. After remaining a short time in its new home, it showed signs of dying, and, in fact, continued to blacken rapidly from the base upwards ; it was sent to me to add to my museum specimens, and I had it placed in a dry brick building. The stem, which had for the most part decomposed and turned black, continued to do so till it had reached the fracture, from which the upper part, instead of mortifying as its lower extremities had done, not only retained its bright green colour, but even took a still brighter green at the apex, by pushing forth a new growth.

"When young, the stems of these plants are very fleshy, and appear outwardly like a solid mass of green succulent matter; as the stems get older, however, an immense quantity of oxalate of lime is formed in them, so much indeed that, if a stem is dried and a section made across it, the grains fall out like so much sand, leaving only the outer cuticle with the spines attached, and the ring of wood which is formed of separate wedge-shaped masses, and situated at about an equal distance between the centre and the circumference of the stem. This was the case with the lower part of the specimen just mentioned, while the upper part had formed roots of its own, which had struck down into the decaying vegetation and oxalate of lime, and so made a fresh start in life.

" *Echinocereus* is another genus which is closely allied to *Cereus*. Between twenty and thirty species are enumerated, the plants of which are all small, about a foot or so in height, with either simple or branched stems, some of which are divided into numerous ribs or ridges, while others have few, some only four; these ridges are very strongly armed with sharp spines. The tube of the flowers, unlike most of the other *Cerei*, is very short.

" The genus *Echinopsis* numbers between twenty and thirty species, all natives of Chili, Bolivia, Mexico, Brazil, and Texas; they were formerly included in the genus *Echinocactus*, but from the position of the flowers being at the side of the stem, and not at the top as in the latter genus, modern authors have placed them with the Cerei.

" *Echinopsis multiplex* will serve as a representative of the genus. It is a plant of nearly globular form, with sharp-angled parallel ribs, and groups of spines arranged along these angles; there are from ten to twelve spines in each group, the central one thicker and longer than the rest. The flowers are very large in proportion to the size of the plant, for while the stem may be not more than six or eight inches high and five inches broad, the flower itself is often as high as the plant, and its diameter as great as its length. The colour is a rose-pink inclining to a deeper tint near the apex of the petals. (See page 87.)

" *Echinocactus* is a genus of some interest, not only on account of the large and showy flowers of

its various species, but also on account of the
grotesque and usually globular form of the plants.
themselves; the stems of some, however, are cylindrical, and others are of an oblong shape, but all are
more or less deeply ribbed, some of the ribs being
broad with round edges, and others acute with sharp
edges, upon which tubercular swellings are frequently
formed, and in some species are very largely
developed, most of them bearing sharp and very stiff
spines arranged in uniform clusters, and often surrounded at their bases by little woolly tufts. The
head-quarters of the *Echinocacti*, like the bulk of the
whole order, is in Mexico, more than half of them
being found in that country, and the rest in different
parts of South America; they love hot and stony
localities where they get little rain, and are exposed
to the full effects of the sun. They bear large and
showy flowers, composed of several rows of floral
leaves, the lower or outer sepals having a simple
scale-like appearance, and the upper ones appearing
by an almost imperceptible transition to pass into
petals. The inner petals are more spread out or
radiating, and the stamens are shorter than the
petals, are indefinite, and are united to the tube of
the calyx. The stigmas are five to ten in number,.
and radiate from the top of a column-like style.
The flowers are produced at or near the top of the
plant, springing from the upper side of the younger
bundles of spines. Perhaps the largest and most
interesting species is *E. helophorus* (*E. visnaga* of

some authors). It has numerous close, sharp, parallel ridges, with clusters of spines arranged along their edges at short distances from each other: so numerous are these spines that a comparatively small plant in the Cactus-house of the Royal Gardens, Kew, some time back, was computed to have upon it not less than 17,600, while a larger specimen in the same house had as many as 51,000. These spines are very long, sharp, and stiff, and are constantly used by the natives for toothpicks, and are said to be very durable. Probably the largest plant of this species ever introduced to this country was one received at Kew some years ago; it weighed one ton, and was nine feet in height by three in diameter. This plant, however, did not live long after its introduction. (See page 48.)

" *Echinocactus cornigerus* has a very singular appearance, being almost entirely encased in spines. The central one of each group is very broad, flattened, and deflexed, and is very strong. Other species are *E. electracanthus*, *E. Pfiefferi*, and *E. ornatus*.

" *Melocactus* is a genus numbering about thirty species, growing in Mexico, Brazil, New Granada, and the West Indies. The species are mostly globular, with more or less prominent ribs, the edges of which are densely clothed with long stiff pines, each tuft being placed at very regular distances; the small flowers are buried in a mass of woolly hairs and fine spines, and are arranged in a cylindrical or hemispherical head at the top of the plant. The *Turk's Cap Cactus* (*Melocactus communis*) is a well-known species, being frequently seen in cultivation in this country. It covers large tracts of land in South America and the West Indies, seldom growing more than two feet high. Owing to the arid nature of the districts in which the plants grow, it is said that the mules, after removing the spines with their feet, suck the juice or water which the plants contain, for the purpose of quenching their thirst. The name of *Turk's Cap Cactus* is derived from the resemblance to a Turk's cap of the red-coloured cylindrical flowering portion. (Fig .5, p. 11.)

"The genus *Mammillaria* is a large and interesting one; it contains a great variety of forms. It derives its name from the fleshy tubercles or mammillæ which cover the whole stem, and which are arranged in a spiral form, varying, however, considerably in size in the different species. It is from the presence of these mammillæ that the members of their genus are readily known from their allies. The flowers, which are of different colours in the several species —some rose-colour, others white, and others yellow —are borne near the tops of the plants, and are arranged in a transverse zone, each flower being sessile at the base of the mammæ.

"Unlike those of many of the *Cerei*, they open in the day and close at night. The fruits are obovate and berry-like, and contain a number of small seeds. The species abound in Mexico, but some are found in Southern California, Texas, and Missouri on the north, Guatemala on the south, and even down to Buenos Ayres and Chili.

"The plants are usually small, but the forms which they assume are most varied: some appear to be composed simply of a series of small, green, fleshy mammillæ, each having almost the appearance of an individual plant, and each being crowned with a tuft of spines; others, again, appear like squat masses of vegetable matter, rising but a few inches high, composed of numerous mammillæ covered with small star-like spines, most beautifully and uniformly arranged. *M. pusilla* is one of this description, and a prettier little plant it is difficult to find, both by reason of the beautiful and delicate arrangement of the spines, the yellow and rose-coloured flowers, and the small, bright, crimson berry-like fruits which succeed them. *M. densa* is another of similar character; the mammæ are, however, rather larger; while in *M. elephantidens* they are larger still, and are partially divided longitudinally by a deep depression; the apices are crowned with six or seven radiating spines. Many other species, having a similar spreading habit, are equally interesting and beautiful, but space will not allow me to mention them.

"Perhaps the tallest species of the whole group is *M. coronaria*, which is one of the cylindrical-growing forms; and though in collections we seldom see it more than twelve inches high, it is said to attain a height of five feet; it has crimson-coloured flowers, and the spines are very uniformly arranged on the mammillæ, being seated in little tufts of white woolly hairs. *M. crucigera* is a very pretty plant, having at the tips of its mammillæ four radiating spines springing from a white, wool-like cushion. *M. Parkinsoni* is another of the cylindrical forms, having long sharp white spines tipped with a reddish brown tinge. In *M. dolichocentra* the mammillæ are long and distinct, capped with four long white spines, not radiating, as in most of the species, but pointing outwards almost in a direct line with the mammillæ. *M. acanthophlegma* is a most beautiful little plant; the mammillæ are small and somewhat pointed at the apex, which is crowned with a delicate series of star-shaped hairs surrounding the small spines.

"Before closing this article a few words must be said about the *Opuntias*, which genus, in an economic point of view, is certainly the most valuable of the entire family, for it is from one or more species of *Opuntia* that the cochineal insect derives its food. About 150 species have been described, but it will be utterly impossible to mention even a tithe of them. The fruits of many are eaten under the name of *Prickly Pears*, and may sometimes be seen exposed for sale in the streets of London. Some are mucilaginous and very insipid, while others have a refreshing and agreeable flavour. They are more or less egg-shaped or pear-shaped, are covered with tufts of small prickles or spines, and at their apex bear a large scar denoting the position of the fallen flower-leaves. They consist of a fleshy pulp, enclosing numerous small seeds.

"The species abound chiefly in Mexico, California, Brazil, Peru, and Chili, a few being also found in the West Indies, and some have become naturalized in various parts of Southern Europe. The plants, which are mostly fleshy, becoming woody as they get old, are either erect or decumbent; the stems and branches are frequently jointed, and mostly flattened; some, however, have unjointed cylindrical stems; they seldom grow to a greater height than ten or twelve feet.

"*Opuntia Tuna* is perhaps the tallest-growing of all the species, attaining sometimes the height of twenty feet, and forming a woody stem with jointed branches; the spines are long and stiff, and are arranged at distant intervals in bundles of from four to six each; the flowers are of a reddish-orange colour, and are composed of numerous sepals and petals, gradually passing one into another, and so undistinguishable. The native habitat of this species extends from Mexico to Quito, but it is also found in the West Indies, and has long been naturalized in Southern Europe, Northern Africa, and Madeira. It is one of the species extensively cultivated in Mexico for rearing the cochineal insect. The fruits are edible, and when ripe they contain an abundance of sweet juice of a rich carmine colour, which is used in Naples for water-colour drawings. In the West Indies it is used to colour confectionery, and in Mexico a favourite beverage is made from it. It is from this rich-coloured juice with which the plants abound that the cochineal insect derives its commercial value.

"*Opuntia cochinillifera*—so called from its being a cochineal-bearing species—is largely cultivated for this purpose; it is, however, now separated from *Opuntia*, and placed in the small genus *Nopalea*. Whole plantations of these *Cacti* exist in Mexico, New Granada, and the Canary Islands; the bulk of our imports, which amount to over 2,000 tons annually, and which realise a price of about £400 per ton, being obtained from the two last-named countries. In the cochineal plantations, which are called Nopaleries, the plants are grown in rows, and are not allowed to attain more than four feet in height. The insect which feeds upon these *Cacti*, and of which countless millions are collected and imported into this country every year, is known to entomologists as the *Coccus cacti* of Linnæus. The female insects are placed upon the plants usually about the month of August, this operation being called sowing. They breed very rapidly, and the young insects grow so fast that in about four months the cochineal harvest commences; this is effected by brushing the insects off the plant into a vessel; they are afterwards killed by immersing them in boiling water, or exposing them in heaps to the sun, and when dry they are ready for exportation.

"As I have before said, the general habit of the stems of the *Opuntias* is jointed, without any apparent centre of growth ; but in *O. brasiliensis* we get the truly arborescent character—a cylindrical stem with regular branches.   In the old branches and stems of some of the species, as *O. Tuna*, a large quantity of net-like woody tissue is formed, which has been made into various ornamental articles, as flower-baskets, vases, and trays, &c.   The spines of the *Opuntias* are exceedingly sharp, some of them, as *O. spinosissimus*, being minutely barbed, not only at the point, but for some considerable distance up the sides, so that if it happens to penetrate the flesh ever so slightly, it requires a much stronger pull to free it than would be supposed.   Some of the species are tolerably hardy.   In the genera *Rhipsalis* and *Pereskia* we have plants differing in general from the rest of the *Cacti.*   In the former the plants are small, fleshy, jointed, and leafless, some having long cylindrical stems, looking like mere green cords ; others angular, and others leafy ; while in *Pereskia* the plants have leaves, some being cylindrical, and others broad, flat, and veined."*

---

* By permission of Messrs. Groombridge, the publishers of the "Student," we give as the frontispiece to this work the plate that accompanied Mr. Jackson's paper on Cacti, which was prepared from a photograph taken by Mr. W. Warwick King from a selected group of Cacti at Kew.

In the "Book of the Garden," by McIntosh :—
we read that succulents seem to place little re-
liance on soil, and grow in the very poorest,
such as sand, gravel, or the débris of decaying
rocks, drawing their nourishment through innume-
rable mouths which cover their whole surface. In
imitation of these conditions in culture, they are
potted in light sandy soil, with a portion of lime
rubbish to render it still more porous; receiving
little water at the roots, but abundance once a-day
overhead, which during the summer should be
administered in the afternoon, in the winter this
is best applied early in the day and also to a less
extent. Many of the splendid hybrid varieties of
Epiphyllum and *Cereus* are grown successfully in
rich, well-drained soil, attaining a large size and
producing abundance of gorgeous blooms. Others
of the same section, particularly *Epiphyllum truncatum*, thrive well when grafted upon any of the
strong upright-growing species of *Cactus;* indeed,
they do better in this way than upon their own roots.
Pereskia aculeata makes an excellent stock for this
operation. It is of rapid growth, and, when trained
over arches, or longitudinally along the roof, and
thickly covered with the various varieties of *Epiphyllum truncatum*, has a fine and novel effect; and
then, when wrought upon the upright-growing *Cereus
speciosissimus, Peruvianus, tetragonus,* &c., may also
be made to form in a few years very fine specimens.
The operation is exceedingly simple, and in the

former case requires only the removal of a thin slice of *Pereskia*, to which a small portion of *E. truncatum* is fitted, and secured by placing a little moss over the bandage of matting, and if placed in a partially-shaded spot adhesion will take place in a week or two. A slit is usually made in the angular parts of the *Cereuses*, and the scion is inserted and secured in the same manner. A plant several feet in height may be covered at once by this means, although a portion of the lower part is usually left uncovered, so as to form the specimen in habit of a tree.

In treating of succulents, Thompson's "Gardener's Assistant" says that the natural habitats of these plants are various, some of them existing in dry, sandy plains, fully exposed to the sun's rays, where every other kind of vegetation is parched up; others on naked volcanic rocks. They are of easy culture, many being propagated by seed, and most of them by cuttings, of which the cut surface should be allowed to get dry before insertion. Most of the free-growing kinds succeed best in a mixture of rich sandy loam and peat or leaf-mould; others that are of slow growth require light sandy loam and brick rubbish; others, again, soil of this description, with the addition of peat. Of such as *Cacti*, for example, only the roots should reach soil of a nutritive character; above them should be a layer of sand, which ought to be kept dry in winter in order to prevent rot. And for the same reason, when the sand becomes charged with impurities, it should be replaced with fresh. The pots ought to be well drained, and the materials decidedly porous. Little water is required by this class of plants as compared with others of the same size, for their surface is adapted for expending but little by evaporation, and the demand for a supply of moisture from the roots is consequently small, hence the bulk of these organs likewise bears a small proportion to that of the rest of the plant. The following are some of the principal genera of succulent plants—*Aloe, Crassula, Cactus, Mammillaria, Cereus, Opuntia, Epiphyllum, Mesembryanthemum, Stapelia, Echeveria,* and *Kalosanthes.*

Mr. McElroy, writing on the culture of the *Cactus,* in the *Gardeners' Magazine* of June, 1866, says :— "Our attention will be directed to their general culture. Commencing with their propagation, this can be done either with cuttings or offsets ; the latter is to be preferred, if obtainable. If by cuttings, let the part heal by laying it in any place that is dry; then insert three cuttings in a large 60-pot filled with a mixture of silver sand and soft loam and a little fine leaf-mould; water sufficiently to settle the soil. After they have rooted, pot them singly into small pots, and as soon as they begin to grow top the plants of the free-growing kinds ; this will cause them to throw up shoots from the bottom. The dwarf varieties do not need this treatment. Continue then to shift them, and train as the pots become filled with roots. I find they do well in a soil equal parts of loam and leaf-mould, with a fourth of lime rubbish and a little silver sand—the whole well incorporated. Before using the leaf-mould destroy all the worms you can see, add plenty of drainage at the bottom of the pot; over the same place a layer of moss or any rough material that will prevent the soil finding its way among the crocks. While in a young state, after potting it would be advisable to keep them in a close, warm, humid atmosphere; this will hasten their growth. Of course their after-potting, when they have arrived at the flowering stage of their growth, must depend on the cultivator's object, whether his accommodation is suitable to large specimens or the contrary. After they have done flowering let them make fresh growth, cutting away previously such shoots as may not be required; when they have completed their growth, put them out of doors in a sunny part of the garden. This will ripen their wood, and assist them in the formation of the future buds. They should be taken indoors by the beginning of September, as heavy rains will injure them; when out let their pots be set on slates or boards, to prevent worms getting into the soil. From November to the beginning of February only keep the soil just moistened; after that they may have a liberal supply, especially when the buds are swelling, but be careful not to saturate the soil, or it will become so soddened that the plant will give evidence of it by its unhealthiness.

"Many of the slow-growing kinds can be grafted with success on *C. speciosissima*, which is simply done by making an incision on the top of the shoot; then fit in the cutting, binding the wound with some bass to exclude the air.

"The following varieties I have proved, having grown them for some years :—

Name.	Observations on Growth.	Colour.
Cactus or Epiphyllum :		
Ackermanni majus ...	Medium size	Scarlet
Andersoni	Ditto	Beautiful intense violet
Rubra cærulea	Ditto	Large flowers, dark crimson, violet centre
Crenatum	Tall, shy flowers	Pure white, very fine
Egertoni	Climbing (var.)	Light red
Jenkinsoni multiflora.	Tall, abundant bloomer	Reddish scarlet
Mallisoni	Climbing (var.)	Purplish crimson
Speciosissima	Tall, free grower; very fine large flowers	Crimson, violet centre
Speciosa	Medium, a very abundant bloomer	Light colour, purple shaded
**Speciosa elegans*	One of the very best growers, dwarf, robust habit	Flesh-coloured flowers
Grandiflora	Medium growth, magnificent large flowers	Cream-coloured
Speciosa grandiflora...	Free growth, abundant bloomer	Reddish-scarlet

* See description of this plant, No. 49, page 106.

By permission of the publishers of the Official Guide to the Royal Gardens at Kew, Messrs. Macmillan, we give the following extracts :—

THE SUCCULENT HOUSE AT KEW

Is two hundred feet long by thirty feet wide, and is devoted principally to those plants of warm and arid countries which are characterised either by excessive succulence of the stem or leaves (the '*plantes grasses*' of the French) or by the converse condition of extreme dryness and rigidity. Most of these are natives of Mexico, Central America, South Africa, and the Canary Islands, and require a similar treatment under cultivation.

The more important groups represented here are the *Cactuses* or *Indian Figs*, succulent *Euphorbias*, *Aloes*, *Agaves*, and other *Amaryllidaceæ*, various *Crassulaceæ* (*Houseleeks*, &c.), *Stapelias* or *Carrion-Flowers*, and some of the larger *Bromeliaceæ*.

The *Cactuses* are natives, almost exclusively, of the New World, from whence the Prickly Pear (*Opuntia Ficus-indica*), now abundantly naturalised in the Atlantic Islands, and generally on the shores of the Mediterranean, where it serves to form impenetrable fences, was originally introduced. Notwithstanding the uncouth and often grotesque forms assumed by the fleshy, leafless, and usually spinose stems of these plants, the flowers are often of great beauty, and in some genera of very large size.

Specimens of *Pereskia*, a genus in which the leaves are developed, may be found at the northern extremity of the house. *P. aculeata* bears an acid fruit resembling the gooseberry, hence called West Indian gooseberry.

The stem varies remarkably in form. The principal types are the Columnar, the Globular, and the Jointed or Lobed. Among the more remarkable of the Columnar group are the species of *Cereus*, represented here by small specimens of the *Old-man Cactus* (*C. senilis*), so called from the long wiry grey hair covering the top of the stem, especially of the younger (!) specimens. (See fig. 56, page 130.)

C. giganteus, closely allied to this species, attains a height of 40 or 50 feet in the table-land of South California. It is the tallest and at the

Fig. 16. Group of Cactaceæ. *a.* Columnar *Cereus*. *b.* Globular *Melocactus*. *c.* Lobed or jointed *Opuntia*. *d.* Leafy *Pereskia*. All reduced.

same time one of the most northern species of *Cereus*. The pulp of its fruit is eatable. The growth of these species is extremely slow, and there is reason to believe that the larger individuals are several hundreds of years old. The fruit is a great source of sustenance to the Mexicans and Indians of the regions where it grows. Conserves and molasses or syrup are made from them, which are preserved during the winter season for future use. The wood at the base of old specimens becomes a perfect hollow cylinder, and from thence upwards to the first branches, instead of being solid, it becomes a reticulated network of bundles of wood continuing the hollow cylinder. These trees in abundance give the landscape a very peculiar appearance.

Numerous representatives of the Globular-stemmed *Cactaceæ* are arranged along the shelves on the eastern side of the house, and larger specimens in the central area near the northern end. The species of *Echinocactus*, so called from their resemblance to the *Echini* (Sea-urchins) of our shores, and the *Mammillarias*, belong to this group. Observe the symmetrical vertical ridges or angles of the stem both of the Globular and Columnar species, crowned at short but regular intervals by tufts of spines (rudimentary leaves), which in some species are very long and rigid ; in *Echinocactus Visnaga*, they serve in Mexico as toothpicks. A plant of this species, which measured $9\frac{1}{2}$ feet in circumference, and weighed one ton, was an inmate of this house in 1846 (*see page* 54).   From injury sustained during its conveyance to England it did not long survive. The tissue of many of these fleshy *Cactaceæ* is remarkably charged with crystalline concretions of oxalate of lime, specimens of which may be seen in the Museum.   Of the Jointed *Cactaceæ*, the best illustrations are the *Opuntias* and *Phyllocacti*.   Specimens of *Opuntia Ficus-indica, O. vulgaris* (the *Cactus Opuntia* of Linnæus) and *O. Tuna*, the " Indian Figs," and their allies are arranged in the central area.   *Opuntia cochinillifera*, one of the species upon which the Cochineal insect feeds, is exhibited with the insect upon it, in a small glass case in the Economic House.

The *Indian Fig* is largely cultivated in Mexico, Brazil, and the Canary Islands for the sake of this insect, furnishing the well-known rich crimson dye, Cochineal, of which upwards of 54,000 cwts. were imported into the United Kingdom in 1871. *O. Tuna* is the only species employed in the Canaries for raising cochineal.   It had existed, however, universally in all the islands long previous to the introduction of the insect, or at least to its becoming an article of commercial importance—a condition indeed of not more than thirty or forty years' standing.   The first introduction of the insect was violently opposed by the country people on the ground of its rendering the *Opuntia* barren.

and injuring the crops of their favourite fruit, called
Figos.

On the roughest lava thrives the Indian or
Prickly Pear, of which the large, cooling fruits are
sold at less than 2d. for thirty. This plant is one of
the most useful presents of the New to the Old
World, as it grows on the poorest and most rocky
soil, where nothing else will vegetate, requiring no
attention, and even its succulent-jointed stems are
greedily devoured by goats.

The species of *Phyllocactus* are frequent in parlour
cultivation; their flowers are extremely beautiful.

Specimens of a singular genus, *Rhipsalis*, the only
genus represented in the Old World (Africa), are
exhibited upon a shelf at the north end of the
house.

The succulent *Euphorbias* (Spurges) are chiefly
collected at the same end of the house. Many of
these, especially African and Canary Island species,
closely simulate the Columnar *Cactaceæ*, having
similarly angled stems and a thick green epidermis.
Note especially *E. canariensis*, a shrub growing 10 to
20 feet in height, frequent upon the exposed rocky
ledges of Teneriffe and other islands of the Canary
group.

A very singular appearance is given to the littoral
mountains, near Santa Cruz, in Teneriffe, by the
round pale green bushes or clumps of *Euphorbia
canariensis*, which are dotted over them in such a

way as to produce a curiously spotty effect, that strikes the eye at a considerable distance.

The *Euphorbia grandidens*, of the Cape of Good Hope, is a singular tree, which forms a remarkable feature in the woods of the eastern part of the Cape Colony and adjacent portions of Caffraria. And of the *Gum Euphorbium* plant of Morocco, *Euphorbia resinifera*:—"The inhabitants of the lower regions of Atlas make incisions in the branches of the plants with a knife, whence the juice issues, which, after being heated by the sun, becomes a substance of a whitish yellow colour, and in the month of September drops off, and forms the gum *Euphorbium*. The plants produce abundantly once only in four years, but this fourth year's produce is more than all Europe can consume ; it being a very powerful cathartic. The people who collect the gum are obliged to tie a cloth over their mouth and nostrils to prevent the small dusty particles from annoying them, as they produce incessant sneezing. The branches of the plant are brought to Mogador, for the use of tanners, by the boats which go from thence to Agadeer, where it abounds, and to it probably the Morocco leather owes its reputed pre-eminence."

Most of the *Spurges* abound in an acrid, milky, often highly poisonous juice, which flows freely on puncture. *E. jacquiniflora, E. splendens,* and *E. Bojeri,* have the leaves immediately enclosing their inconspicuous flowers coloured a brilliant scarlet.

The *Portulacaria Afra* is the " Spekboom " of the Cape of Good Hope, said to be the favourite food of the elephant. It is one of the numerous forms which confer a peculiar physiognomy on the vegetation of the Colony :—

" The strange, stiff, gaunt forms of the leafless *Euphorbias*, which suggest the idea of some monstrous Indian idols ; the *Aloes*, with their spear-like leaves and tall scarlet spikes ; the pale-green foliage of the Spekboom ; the *Crassulas*, covered with milk-white blossoms ; *Cotyledon*, with its bluish leaves and bright red flowers, form a combination extremely interesting, which must strike every traveller of ordinary habits of observation, by its dissimilarity to anything that is to be seen in other countries. There cannot indeed be a vegetation more peculiar or of a more marked character.

Adjoining the *Cactaceæ* and *Spurges*, in the central area, are the *African Aloes*, characterised by their densely tufted succulent leaves, terminating the stems, from which are thrown up long terminal spikes of showy flowers. The drug Aloes is the inspissated bitter and acrid juice of the fleshy leaves of several species of this genus ; amongst the rest *A. socotrina* (Socotrine), *A. vulgaris* (Barbadoes) and *A. spicata*, and allies (Cape Aloes).

Resembling the *Aloes* in habit are the so-called *American Aloes* — species of *Agave* and *Fourcroya* ; some magnificent examples occupy the southern central area of the house.

"There were two ancient specimens of *Fourcroya gigantea* in the greenhouse (Royal Gardens, Kew, 1844) which had shown no symptoms of flowering till the summer of that year, when each was seen to produce a flowering stem, which grew at first most rapidly. So precisely did the twin plants keep pace with each other that at the very time it was found necessary to make an aperture in the glass roof of the house for the emission of one panicle (26 feet from the ground), a similar release was needed by the other."

The flowers of these plants are borne in branched panicles upon tall terminal stems, often 20 feet or more in height, which grow up from the centre of a huge tuft of leaves, and continue, while at the same time they terminate, the leafy axis. The flowers differ from those of the true *Aloes* in having the ovary adherent and thus apparently below the whorls of the flower. The *American Aloe* rarely flowers in England, though on the shores of the Mediterranean, where it is abundantly naturalised, its tall withered flowering stems often stand "as thick as the masts of small vessels in a harbour." In Mexico this species is very abundant, and of great value to the mountain population, who are supplied by it with a beverage (Pulque), obtained by tapping the succulent axis of the central bunch of leaves previous to flowering. A useful fibre also is furnished by the leaves. The huge sword-like fleshy leaves of some of the larger specimens of *Agave* and *Fourcroya* average 12 lbs. in weight. (See Fig. 30, p. 103.)

We take the following from the *Gardeners' Chronicle* of March 1st, 1845 :—

"THE MONSTER CACTUS AT KEW.

"The 4th of January, 1845, number of the *Illustrated London News* contained a figure and short description of a gigantic *Cactus* that was presented, with many others, to the Royal Gardens of Kew by Frederick Staines, Esq., of San Luis, Potosi. It has been named, in compliment to that liberal and public-spirited gentleman, *Cactus (Echinocactus) Stainesii.*

"Before giving an idea of the size and weight of the *Viznaga,* our readers may feel interested in knowing something of the difficulties that have attended the procuring these huge specimens of the *Cactus* tribe, and how much the man of science and the public generally are indebted to Mr. Staines for his great exertions, by which this country came into possession of such curiosities; this is best told in that gentleman's own words, contained in a letter dated August 20th, 1844. He writes to the Director of the Royal Gardens at Kew :—' Now that we have been successful in getting the pink-spined *Cactus (Echinocactus Stainesii*) in safety to England, I am increasingly solicitous to despatch one of the monsters which I mentioned before. But it cannot be *that monster* which I have so long kept in my possession here, always hoping to send him to Kew; for, I regret to say, it began to decline near the root last month, probably on account of the great weight, and not being put sufficiently deep into the ground. I mean, however, to have another deposited in a strong box, sending the box first to the mountain where the monsters grow, and placing it on the springs of a carriage which I shall despatch for that purpose, and so forward it to Vera Cruz. My monster friend cannot travel any other way, from its stupendous size and immense ponderosity, which cannot be adequately calculated for here, where the largest machine for the purpose of conveying weights does not pass 400 lbs. And this enormous plant will require twenty men at least to place it upon the vehicle, with the aid of such levers as our Indians can invent upon the occasion. This *Cactus* grows in the deep ravines of our loftiest mountains, amongst huge stones ; the finest plants are inaccessible to wheeled vehicles, and even on horseback it is difficult to reach them. Still I shall use my utmost endeavours to get at a large one, and shall cause the palm mats to be sewed most carefully round its huge and thorny circumference, before applying to its roots the crowbars destined to wrench it from its resting-place of unknown centuries. It will have to travel 300 leagues, and happy shall I be if I hear that the carriage has not broken down between this city and Mexico, through which capital it must pass on its way to Vera Cruz. These monsters are of a dark green colour, with formidable black spines, three inches long.'

E

" On the 20th October Mr. Staines writes :—' The monster would, ere this time, have been on the road to Vera Cruz ; but, on sending for it, the answer was returned that it measured two *varas* in length (the *vara* is a trifle less than one English yard), and as my descriptions had led you to expect one of larger size, I was concerned to find that the individual in question could not come up to your expectations, and therefore I have succeeded in finding another, and hope to have the pleasure, ere closing this letter, of communicating its safe arrival here, for the specimen has been already seven days on the road to this place, in a large, clumsy, two-wheeled waggon, drawn by eight oxen. Every care shall be bestowed upon its packing, my chief anxiety being that the specimen shall reach you in a fresh state, and meet with no detention in Mexico. I trust to get it shipped at Vera Cruz by the packet of the 1st of December. Eight strong mules, if these be found sufficient, will drag it to Mexico, and thence to Vera Cruz, and no time shall be lost upon the road, twelve days being allowed for reaching the capital. It is a great pity that the high mountains between this town and Tampico forbid my sending it by that route, which is but half the distance of the way through Mexico.'

" In a letter to Mr. Parkinson, dated two days later, Mr. Staines says :—' The axle of the cart or waggon in which it was coming had given way near this place, and my servant is to go off to-morrow to replace the damage with a new one. He informs me that two *Cacti* are on the way; one of them, having dark spines, which I shall designate as the Monster, is the heaviest, and measures about three varas in length; the other, with ruby-coloured spines, is very long, and belongs to the same species as that formerly transmitted to Kew.'

"And, lastly, Mr. Staines writes to the following effect, on the 23rd November last:—'I had the pleasure, by the packet Avon, to apprise you of the near arrival of the Monster *Cactus;* but when I saw it my disappointment was grievous—it was so old, the upper part alone being green, and having a healthy appearance. Thus, I instantly decided to send for another, although of probably inferior size. The delay thus incurred may possibly prevent the specimen from reaching Vera Cruz in time for shipment on the 1st of December, as it only left this city for Mexico twelve days ago. My Mexican correspondent assures me that if the mules are not in too exhausted a condition, he will despatch them with the carriage at once; so that they will arrive at Vera Cruz in ten days from Mexico, and possibly give the Monster a chance of going by the same conveyance as carries this letter. Along with it I sent a box, containing a red-spined *Cactus*, about one and a half yard long, which is the very long one which the people mentioned having brought for me. It was too heavy for a mule, so I forwarded it also to Vera Cruz. The Monster now sent is quite green and healthy, and though not standing quite so high as that promised, it makes up for what it lacks in length by its great rotundity.   Fourteen men were required to place it upon the carriage that was despatched to fetch it, which may afford some notion of its weight.'

"On Saturday, February 15th, 1845, the *Cactus* last mentioned, together with five large boxes filled with other individuals of the same tribe, and rarities of different kinds, reached the Botanic Gardens in a condition of security and vigour which are quite remarkable, considering their bulk and weight, the vast overland journey mainly performed through a country of high mountains and perilous roads, and their arrival in our island during one of the severest frosts that had been experienced for many winters. The monster *Cactus* or *Viznaga* (for to it we must confine our attention), as Mr. Staines states in his letter, was too large for a box.   It was first surrounded with a dense clothing of the Spanish moss —a better covering could not have been devised— and well corded.   Fifteen mats, each as large and as thick as an ordinary door-mat, and composed of the fibres of a palm sewn together, formed the exterior envelope.   Freed from these incumbrances, the monster *Viznaga* was seen as perfect, as green, and as uninjured as if it were that morning removed from its native rocks, the very long flagelliform roots arranged in coils, like the cable of a ship.   Ten of our strongest men with difficulty placed it in scales, brought into the garden for the purpose, with a view to ascertain its precise weight, and afterwards, with still greater difficulty, transferred it, perfectly unharmed, to another tub, prepared with suitable soil. There it now stands, surrounded by others of its scarcely less interesting fellow *Cacti*, the gifts of Mr. Staines and Mr. Parkinson. The weight of the *Viznaga* is 713 lbs. ; height from the surface of the earth, 4½ ft. ; measured over the top, from the ground on each side, 10 ft. 9 in. ; circumference at 1 ft. from the ground, 8 ft. 7 in. ; number of deep angles or costæ, 44.

"As a species, although belonging to the same genus, *Echinocactus*, as *E. Stainesii*, it is quite distinct, and appears altogether unknown to authors. Its nearest affinity is certainly with a species introduced by Mr. Parkinson, and known in our gardens (on account of its being used in Mexico, boiled down with sugar and eaten as a conserve) under the name of *E. edulis*. Specifically, however, it is perfectly distinct, and it seems to be just that its native appellation should be preserved ; a name, too, not inappropriate, if we rightly understand the meaning of it, as applied by the Spaniards. *Viznaga* or *Visnaga*, or *Bisnaga*, is a corruption of *Bisacuta* (twice-pointed or sharpened at both ends), and is given by the Spanish to a species of *Daucus* (or *Ammi*) called *Daucus Visnaga*, the rays of whose umbels are employed as picktooths, and in Italy they are handed round the table to the guests. The spines of the *Cactus* are applied to a similar purpose in the warm parts of America.   Upon our plant Mr. John Smith has counted forty-four angles or costæ, and on every angle are fifty fascicles of spines, and four spines compose each fascicle.   Thus there are 8,800 spines or picktooths—enough for the supply of a whole army of even such hungry soldiers as the Trojan followers of Æneas."

This *Cactus* died, and another, much larger, was brought to Kew Gardens the following year.   It was nine feet in height, and rather more than three feet in diameter, and weighed one ton; but this also lived but a short time.   The roots must, we suppose, have been greatly injured from the force employed to wrench them up from the earth.

Mr. Shirley Hibberd, in the " Amateur's Greenhouse," speaking of *Mammillaria, Melocactus, Echinocactus, Cactus*, and *Cereus*, says it is a mistake to grow them in brick rubbish.   They require a mixture of equal parts of turfy loam and leaf mould; and if the last is not to be had, fibry peat must be mixed up with the loam, and about a fourth part of the whole bulk of silver sand added; they may stand in the same pot three years.   It is a risk to employ manure.   The best time to repot is from March to May.   When a *Cactus* is turned out of a pot, remove the old soil from the roots, and repot firmly, the base of the plant slightly elevated, so that the earth will slope down from it all round, and steady it with a few sticks, thrust in so as to prevent it toppling over.   If there is any difficulty in getting the roots into the pot without crowding them, cut away all the smaller and any of the larger ones that appear to be dying. The *Cotyledon* should be potted in sandy compost. About a sixth part of old mortar of the size of peas may be added with advantage. They appear to live by their leaves more than by their roots. In the *Gardener's Magazine* Mr. Hibberd gives the following list of a few most desirable to those about to form a collection :—

Mammillaria atrata.	Melocactus depressus.	Echinocactus imbricatus.
Andræa.	Grengelii	latispinus.
carnea.	macracanthus.	Mackieanus.
cirrhifera.	polycanthus.	montevidensis.
spinis fuscis.	pyramidalis.	parvispinus.
coronaria.	Sellowii.	platyacanthus.
depressa.	Cereus affinis.	scopa spinis albis.
fulvispina.	cæsius.	subgibbosus.
Karwinskii.	tenuispinus.	tenuispinus.
magnimamma.	undatus.	tubiflorus.
quadrispina.	Echinocactus densus.	Cactus corrugatus.
sphacelata.	echinatus.	reductus or nobilis.
Wildiana.	Eyresii.	senilis.
	Gilliesii.	

Another writer in the same periodical says :— " As regards the winter treatment, there is a fallacy current that often causes the death of a rare kind, and that is that they do not require water for six or seven months of the year. Many a gardener would anathemise his young men for watering them later than October or earlier than the end of March ; whereas, if kept in the right temperature, they enjoy an occasional dose of water all the year round. There is not the slightest occasion for keeping them a whit drier than a good show geranium-grower keeps his plants during the dull weeks of mid-winter. But they must be kept in a dry, warm greenhouse, and in the warmer part of it, near the glass. Cold or hard frost is fatal to a great many species. They rot off after a degree of cold which New Holland plants bear with impunity, and should, as a rule, never be kept in a house where the temperature sinks below the freezing-point, or, to be on the healthful side, say 40°. I have seen many rare kinds, including the beautiful *Mammillaria senilis*, killed by frost. Nothing can exceed the beauty of its white pellucid but dangerously-hooked spines. Some of the *Mammillarias* assume the cockscomb form. These are grafted on some of the *Cereus* tribe in the way of hexagonus, and thus you may see many symmetrical green and fluted shafts crested with a white and densely spiny cockscomb of *Mammillaria*, which grows stronger on the *Cereus* than on its own roots, and forms one of the most striking plants in existence. Then, again, there are normal forms of the same kinds grafted on cylindrical stems of green *Cacti*, and forming a jutting round spiny nob on the end of the little green shaft, and putting it almost out of sight when looked down upon. Only fancy some of such with a corona of crimson buds—perhaps succeeded by bright scarlet fruit! Many *Gasterias*, *Haworthias*, and *Apicras*, for instance, are remarkably neat and singular in their habit. Some of the *Euphorbias*, *too*—particularly the globular *Euphorbias*, that sit on the pot like little melons placed on the soil, and are furnished with spines big enough for a Gleditschia —are most extraordinary. Then there is *Echeveria metallica* and others, not to speak of such tiny and miscellaneous pets as *Monanthes polyphylla*, some of the *Crassulas* with pink margined glaucous leaves, the ciliated and tabuliform *Sempervivums*, and a host of even greater beauty. I may add, for the benefit of indoor gardeners, that some of the dwarf *Aloes* and *Gasterias* will not only grow, but flower, in a warm room, or even in a dark kitchen window.

EUPHORBIA (ALSO CALLED SPURGE).

Loudon remarks that this is named from Euphorbus, physician to Juba, King of Mauritania —the former having first used this plant in medicine. This is a genus of grotesque and curious plants, few of them of either beauty or use. They are all milky, mostly herbacious; several, however, are shrubby, upright for the most part, very few creeping; some are leafless, but most of them are leafy. Stems angular or tubercled, or more frequently cylindrical or columnar; unarmed, or, in the angular sorts, resembling the upright *Cactuses*, and armed with prickles, which are either solitary or in pairs, placed in a single row on the top of the ridges. The *Euphorbia officinarum*, like a *Torch Cactus*, with one or two other plants of this genus, furnish the Euphorbium of medicine. In the lower regions of Mount Atlas the people collect the con-creted gum resin, which they call furbiune, in September. It is obtained by making slight incisions in the branches of the plant with a knife, from which a milk-like juice exudes, and forms into tears of an oblong or roundish form. The succulents of this family thrive the better if a little lime rubbish be added to their sandy loam.

MESEMBRYANTHEMUM.

We again quote from "Loudon's Encyclopædia of Plants":—"*Mesembryanthemum* is taken from the Greek signifying the mid-day, as the flowers usually expand at that time; the termination anthemum signifies flowering. The species of this extensive genus are singular, yet beautiful, and some even splendid plants. Their leaves are of odd shape, and the habits of most of the sorts slovenly and insignificant, though some are grotesque; but the flowers make ample amends by their profusion, and the brilliancy of their colours, and the length of time the species continue in flower. Most of them are perennial. Most of the species are so hardy, that on dry rock-work, in a sheltered part of the garden, they will endure ordinary winters. Everything, however, depends on keeping them dry. The dwarf kinds require but little water, and to be grown in small pots in a very sandy or gravelly soil. They should be kept quite dry when in a dormant state;

but when growing freely, and at the flowering season, they require a moderate supply of water."

Mr. Hibberd, in the "Garden Oracle" (1864), remarks :—"Though of this family there are hundreds of species in cultivation, and many of them nearly alike, the amateur will find it the most entertaining of all the families of succulents, and one in which he may multiply examples to almost any extent without becoming weary. Our own collection comprises only 125 species, yet among these we have some in bloom every day throughout the year. All they require is a sandy soil, plenty of drainage, plenty of sun, little water in winter, and to be put out of doors from June to October. Many are quite hardy, and invaluable for rockwork."

In Grindon's Botany we read that the *Mesembryanthemum tigrinum* (often mis-called the Rose-of-Jericho, and still more foolishly the "Resurrection" flower), are imported from the Cape of Good Hope as curiosities. When dry, they resemble a round gray button, about an inch in diameter, but on being dipped in water, they expand into a beautiful star, the rays consisting of the carpels, which then discharge their small beach seeds. As the moisture evaporates, the button-form is resumed.

CRASSULACEÆ—The stone-crop family.

THE GENUS SEDUM.

It is remarked in Grindon's "Botany" that, sprinkled all over the world, the 300 known species of the stone-crop family are remarkable for growing on sun-scorched rocks and naked walls, on roofs and sandy plains, such as other plants could not endure for a day ; and, though many are rooted in the earth, it is not that they require the soil as a source of nutriment, but simply as anchorage. They take their food almost entirely through the pores of the leaves—their delicate mouths invisible to the naked eye. Nothing is more extraordinary than to see the little *Sedum acre* sitting in golden epaulettes on the tops of mountain walls, exposed to the hottest rays of the noontide sun, and flourishing most when they come earliest and stay the longest. The red *Orpine* will live for months, suspended by a string, without being once supplied with water ; indeed, it is said that it will even grow freely after being placed between papers and pressed for the herbarium.

Loudon says that the word *Sedum* is taken from the Latin word *sedere*, to sit—these plants, growing on the bare rocks, look as if sitting upon it. The species are low succulents, some of them pretty, others curious. They seem destined by nature to clothe rocks and dry arid plains, after a certain portion of vegetable soil has been generated by lichens and mosses.

SEMPERVIVUM.—The House-leek family.

Sempervivum, from *semper vivere*, to live for ever, in allusion to the tenacity of life common to plants of this genus. See Nos. 11, 23, 51, &c., in the description of the plants in our case.

THE CULTIVATION OF CACTI.

BY J. CROUCHER.

From the " Student."

CULTIVATION OF CACTI.—In written instruction on the cultivation of any class of plants, there are many points of detail one can scarcely put into words; which points must be learned by observation in practice; but the general conditions of success may be, such as composts, temperature of house, propagation, time and mode of potting, &c., which instructions, if well followed out, will be sure to lead to good cultivation.

The majority of the genera are sun-loving subjects, and as a consequence the first thing to be taken into consideration, is to get your house so situated as to ensure the greatest amount of direct light; the best aspect will be due south; a lean-to house is the best, with good clear glass, to which the plants must be as near as possible; the genera Epiphyllum and Rhipsalis, are exceptions to this rule, and prefer a little shade in the summer, as they mostly grow in the forests, but in any house there are always some parts more in the shade than others; the plants are not damaged by the sun, but will grow more luxuriantly in the shade. It is not easy to get the house too hot for Cacti in the summer, but they will thrive well in a temperature of 60° to 80° with sun, and in winter the majority will bear a minimum of 40° with dry air ; though the genera Rhipsalis and Epiphyllum must be kept at 55° to 65°, or they will protest by looking very yellow. Most of these plants being natives of those parts of America lying south of the equator, they, as a consequence, get their warmest season when we get our coldest, which gives them a tendency to grow during our winter ; and a predilection for rotting if not kept perfectly dry. As above stated, the whole of these plants being American, they should not be repotted in early spring, as is the common practice ; which practice seems to have originated from the fact of most plants starting into growth on or about that time. I have often thought, that if amateurs and gardeners were to think more on this subject, they would at once see the folly of supposing that all countries had their spring at the same time as we have in England ; it matters little with most persons if the plants come from East, West, North, or South, they must be potted in our spring ; and as the plants will not grow out of their season, the soil gets stale, and when the roots do begin to grow, they find the condition unfavourable, and the result is stunted growth, and sometimes death ; not through a wrong compost, but unseasonable potting. The potting of *Cacti* should be left until June or July, when they will be on the point of starting into growth. The best compost is loam, with silver sand and broken bricks, the quantity of sand must be regulated by the stiffness or otherwise of the loam ; the object being to make the whole sufficiently porous for the water to pass through freely; as a rule one gallon of sand to three bushels of loam, and one bushel of finely broken bricks will suit for the genera Opuntia, Echinocactus, Echinopsis, Cereus, and Mammillaria; for Epiphyllum and Rhipsalis, a mixture of rough peat and loam, with a little sand and rough crocks, is the best. Such as *R. cassytha*, *funalis*, *saglionis*, and *mesembryanthoides* may be grown on pieces of fern stems, in baskets or pots suspended the same as Orchids, and very interesting objects they make; *Cereus flagelliformis* and *leptopes* succeed best suspended in a pot, with the ordinary soil: *C. grandiflorus*, *Macdonaldiæi*, and the other night-flowering species, grow best planted in the back border of a stove with a tolerable amount of moisture in the air; it is not necessary to give them much soil, as they get most of their nourishment from their aerial- roots. When the plants are to be potted, the whole of the small fibres of the roots should be cut off; this is a very particular point in the cultivation of this class of plants, as it enables you to get the plants into small pots, and if left on they decay, and so do more harm than good, by making the soil impure; amateurs, as a rule, are very shy at cutting the roots from their plants, but a good cultivator of Cacti has not the least hesitation about the subject, and it is probable that they lose most of their fibrous roots during the dry season, in their native habitat; the soil should be made quite firm in the pot and well drained, taking care to put enough rough lumps of soil on the drainage to prevent the soil from getting amongst it, and so defeat the object for which it is placed there. Manure should be specially avoided, as it will cause the soil to get charged with impurities, with the least excess of water, which impurities the plants will take up, and though they may look green and healthy, may some day be found quite dead; some persons recommend manure, but after sad experience, I say away with it. I also know persons who grow their plants in nearly all manure, but they are grown for sale, and their profit consists in the death of the same. Others, again, recommend lime rubbish being mixed with the soil; which practice has originated from the fact of oxalate of lime being found to constitute a great portion of the substance of these plants, but lime rubbish from the debris of old buildings is very different from that found in the natural soil of the plants, and the effect on the roots is to cause them to become stunted, and what horticulturists called clubbed; therefore my advice is, if you want your plants to grow well don't use lime rubbish.

When the plants have been potted they should be kept without water until they show signs of growth; never mind if they don't ask for it until two or three months after potting; don't give it them until they do, for they always contain enough moisture to enable them to start, and until that start is made, the roots have not begun to grow; when the plants have started into growth they may be watered about once a week, for the first month; after that twice, with a good syringing every other evening before shutting the house. This treatment may be continued until the end of August, when the syringe must be laid aside; after September, the watering must not be oftener than once in fourteen days; from October till March, the genera Mammillaria, Echinocactus, Cereus, and most of the Opuntias must be kept quite dry. As the Phyllocacti flower in the early spring, they must get water about once a month during the winter. Epiphyllum and Rhipsalis may be moderately dry, but they will not endure so much drought as their more succulent allies. It is not necessary to pot the plants every season, as they like to be pot bound; some do well in the same pot for five or six years. Should any plant be found to have lost its roots, or show signs of decay, the infected part should be cut clean out at once, and the plant turned up to the full power of the sun, till it begins to show fresh roots, when it may be repotted, and watered with care; this rule of turning the plants up to the sun should be especially attended to with newly imported plants, as they require all superfluous moisture cleared from them; their roots should be cut off, as when dead they act like string, conducting moisture to the plants; to the neglect of cutting off the dead roots, I attribute the many failures to grow the Turk's Cap Cactus (*Melocactus communis*), although this species evidently does not

F

increase in size after forming the cap or flowering point, yet it may be kept alive some years.

MODES OF PROPAGATION.—The genera Rhipsalis, Phyllocactus, Cereus, and Opuntia are easily increased by cuttings, which should be taken off in May, and laid in the sun until rooted, when they should be potted and watered carefully, though Rhipsalis and Phyllocactus may be potted at once, and kept dry about fourteen days, when they will be rooted and may be watered; Echinocactus and Mammillaria must be increased by offsets; Echinocactus requires the top to be cut off, which must be exposed to the sun until rooted, the old plant will throw out young ones which may be taken off the next season; as a rule the Echinocactus is slow in throwing offsets, and care must be taken not to let the plant get any water until it shows signs of doing so; patience is a virtue in great demand in the propagation of this section of the order. The slender growing species are often grafted on stronger and faster growers, though care must be taken not to select for a stock one as celebrated for vigour as the scion is for want of it, or your labour will be in vain; as a stock for the smaller growing Echinocacti, *Cereus tortuosus*, or *colubrinus*, are the best; for the larger, *C. peruvianus* and *gemmatus*. In grafting, care must be taken to cut the two ends rather convex than concave, as they are apt to shrink a little, which would cause a separation, and so spoil the graft; the scion must be tied firmly to the stock, taking care that the edges meet, or at least one of them; the best plan to ensure against accidents is to put three sticks into the pot, and tie them together above the plant, thus causing a continual pressure from above. In grafting *Opuntia clavarioides* you may cut a cuneiform notch in the stock, and cut the scion to fit tightly, keep them firm with a stick on each side, and a thorn run through the graft. Some of the smaller species of Cereus, as *C. tuberosa* may be made pointed, with a corresponding hole in the stock; in all cases taking care not to disturb the plant when once grafted. When the operation is finished, the plant must be put into a close frame, or the shadiest part of the house, until it is out of danger. Epiphyllums are generally grafted, but not necessarily. The common stock used is *Pereskia grandifolia*, and *Blea*, but *Cereus speciosissimus*, and *triangularis*, make very good stocks, these plants being stouter, and more in proportion to the scion, though Pereskia stocks are more to be depended upon than Cereus. Cuttings of Pereskias intended for stocks should be put in in spring, selecting the young straight shoots of the previous season, about six inches long, or according to fancy; about September is the best season for grafting Epiphyllums. The scion should consist of one or two joints; cut the outer bark off about one inch on each side of the scion, split the stock about the same length, put the scion in, and tie or pin it with a thorn, according to which stock you use; the plants must then be put into a close frame, and laid on their sides until united, which they will do in about six weeks, when they may be stood upright and gradually hardened off. Most of the species may be raised from seed, which should be sown as soon as collected, if possible, and put into a temperature of 60°. The young plants grow very slowly at first; when potted off they should be placed near the light; it is best to let them remain in the seed pot until the following season, as they are very apt to damp if they are potted off too soon. Seed collected abroad should be left in the pulp, which being its natural protector prevents the air acting on it, and drying it up; packed in a small tin box it may be sent any distance without losing its vitality. The best flowering varieties are *Cereus speciosissimus*, and its varieties, as *C. Ackermanni, Jenkinsoni, splendens*, and others; these are the forms most commonly grown in cottage windows; the genera Phyllocactus, and Cereus produce many fine flowering varieties.

HYBRIDISATION.—This may be performed by any person, as the stamen and pistils are so very distinct, and the pollen produced in abundance; which may be preserved for some time if kept in a bottle hermetically sealed. I have not met with any successful attempt to cross Mammillaria with Echinocactus, or Opuntia with Cereus, though I know of no cause why they may not be, as the differences in the flowers are not differences of structure, but merely degrees of development; such as a greater or lesser number of stamens and petals, or in the absence in some and length in others of the tube of the corolla, excepting that it may be that the pollen tubes might be too strong for the distance they have to grow from the apex of the stigma, or *vice versa*.

The chief points to be observed in the above directions are, the light, time, and mode of potting, taking special care not to be afraid to cut off the roots. The watering which should be given with a rose on the pot; when given, let it be enough to thoroughly soak the soil; it is best to hold the pot as high as you can, so that the water may fall on all parts of the plant, which serves the double purpose of washing and watering at the same time. Be sure to give them a good drying in the winter, upon which depends the success in flowering them the next season.

Some few species, as *Opuntia vulgaris*, and *Rafinesquiana*, and *Echinopsis Eyriesii*, are hardy in the south of England, and I have no doubt that many species of Opuntia and Echinopsis would do very well in cold frames in winter and the open air in summer. For an amateur the Cacti are the best class of plants to cultivate, as they offer the greatest scope for number of species, and require so little attention. In a house twenty feet by twelve, from 400 to 500 species may be grown; in the summer the house can be left night and day with air, and if the owner had no person he could trust, he might lock the house and leave them a week at a time without fear of harm; in the winter, if he should be obliged to leave home, the only thing would be to get the heat looked after, and his pets would welcome him home with as fresh an appearance as when he left. One often hears the remark from some person who has been disappointed—"I bought some in the market, but they soon died;" the fact is these plants are newly potted, and should be treated as advised for fresh potted plants. Cacti intended for exportation to long distances should be laid in the sun until they begin to shrivel, when they should be packed in some coarse material, as straw, taking care to use enough to prevent the spines of one piercing the other, for if one begins to rot, the whole will become moist, and endanger the whole cargo; holes must be made in the sides of the boxes to cause a current of air to pass through, as a safeguard against accident.

SELECT SUCCULENTS FOR AMATEURS.
By J. CROUCHER, from the *Gardener's Magazine,* August, 1876.

The first requisite for successful attempts with these, as with all other plants, is to have a proper house, for though they are easily grown they are a little peculiar in their requirements, and a suitable house is a matter of the first importance. If I purposed growing a small collection I should build a small span-roofed house with a central stage and side tables. If I only purposed growing dwarf sorts the central stage should be of the step form, not flat, because such things as *Gasterias* and *Haworthias* are best with a partial shade, therefore they could be put on the north side. The heating apparatus should be arranged so that the ordinary greenhouse temperature may be maintained.

The soil I find best is light loam with plenty of sand and brickrubbish. I never use peat. Some cultivators use leaf-mould, but I do not find it good. The spring is the best season for potting, as as well for purchasing plants. Cuttings of *Cacti*, *Aloes*, and *Gasterias*, are best laid up to the sun a few days or weeks, according to their state of moisture, before potting, but *Stapelias*, *Crassulas*, *Mesembryan-themums*, and *Sempervivums*, should be put in at the time of cutting them off, and left a few days before watering. If put on a shelf near the glass, all the better.

In watering succulents, more especially Cacti and the Aloe tribe, never give any unless the plant is quite dry ; but in saying this, I hope that no one will suppose they require starving. There is a great difference in giving a plant water when dry, and in watering periodically by the almanac and the clock. By practice you may see by the appearance of the plants when they want water, as well as you can a Fuchsia, or, indeed, any other plant. If the skin of a Cactus, Aloe, or Gasteria shines, and it feels very plump to the touch, there is no water wanted. Indeed, if you give it, you may find some time after the whole thing collapsed. I have fed such things as *Mesembryanthemum tigrinum* and *M. obcordellum* until the epiderm has bursted, and then they perished; but during July and August they may be syringed freely.

I should always advise amateurs to begin with one genus, and endeavour to complete it. By adopting this course more pleasure is derived, and more real knowledge gained; for when once a man has mastered the varieties of one genus he has got a key to nature's plans, and will really know more than the man who is familiar with a few of twenty genera.

In starting a collection it is best to get small plants and grow these on, for there is much more pleasure in noting the gradual development of a plant from a mere mite to a finely-developed specimen.

Among *Cacti*, the *Mammillaria*, *Echinocactus*, and *Echinopsis*, are the most beautiful for small specimens. The tall-growing *Cereus* are so apt to get to the top of the house too soon, and *Opuntias* are not very comely. The night-flowering *Cereus* do not prosper well in a greenhouse. But all the three genera named above are perfectly safe if kept from frost.

The following are the most easily procured and beautiful species of

ECHINOCACTUS.

Myriostigma.	*Mamillosus.*	*Camellosous.*
Ottonis.	*Scopa.*	*Monvillii.*
Tortuosa.	*Scopa cristata.*	*Tabularis.*
Longihamatus.	*Recurvus.*	*Macrodiscus.*
Sinuatus.	*Denudatus.*	*Ingens.*
Gibbosus.	*Williamsii.*	*Corynoides.*
Courantii.	*Cumingii.*	

Of the *Echinopsis* all are beautiful large-flowering plants easily grown, and almost hardy. I have had them exposed to ten degrees of frost without harm. The following are desirable species of

ECHINOPSIS.

Multiplex.	*Zuccariniana.*	*Rohlandii.*
Eyriesii.	*Zuccariniana rosea.*	*Pentlandii.*
Oxygonus.	*Sellowi.*	*Valida.*
	Decaisniana.	

The species of *Mammillaria* are all easily grown, and are moderately hardy. They do not like a close atmosphere at any time, and small plants should be near the glass. If so placed, and enjoying plenty of air, they will stand any amount of sun light. They vary much in colour of spines, so I have arranged them in sets of yellow, white, and red spined varieties. The following are the best among the many species of

MAMMILLARIA.

RED-SPINED.	WHITE-SPINED.	YELLOW-SPINED.
Caracasana.	*Nivea.*	*Auriceps.*
Decipiens.	*Bicolor.*	*Densa.*
Discolor.	*Parkinsoni.*	*Stella aurata.*
Elgeans.	*Gracilis.*	*Wildiana.*
Hermannii.	*Peacocki.*	*Sulphurea.*
Pentacantha.	*Digitalis.*	*Rhodantha.*
Spinosissima.	*Angularis.*	*Echinarta.*
Preciosa.	*Cirrhifera.*	*Dolichocentra.*
Pusilla.	*Crucigera.*	
Sphacelata.	*Conopsea.*	
	Formosa.	
	Senilis.	

MAMMILLARIA WITH LARGE YELLOW FLOWERS.

Elephantidens.	*Longimamma.*	*Radians.*
Sulcolonata.	*Sphærica.*	*Scolymoides.*
	Pycnacantha.	

This list might be lengthened easily, for our collections are rich in fine species of this genus, but a longer list might confound instead of guide usefully.

CEREUS.—This genus is composed of tall plants that are easier to manage than the globular Cacti. Many are grand in flower, especially the night blooming species, as they are generally denominated; but all the Cereus open their flowers in the evening, and but few last until the middle of the next day. All the trailing or climbing forms require a stove temperature to bring them to perfection. It is a sure sign of a Cereus being of tropical origin if it emits aerial roots.

CEREUS FOR THE STOVE.	CEREUS FOR THE GREENHOUSE.
Grandiflora.	*Pruinosus.*
Macdonaldiæ.	*Strigosus.*
Lehmanni.	*Multangularis.*
Quadrangularis.	*Pueruvianus monstrosus.*
Nycticallis.	*Glaucus.*
Humilis.	*Azureus.*
Pterogonus.	*Chilensis.*
Longihamatus.	*Candicans.*
	Tweedii.

OPUNTIA is a rough genus, but there are a few very good plants among them, of which are the following :—

OPUNTIA.		
Andicola.	*Currassavica.*	*Exuviata.*
Clavarioides.	*Maxima.*	*Polyantha.*
Clavarioides cristata.	*Cylindrica.*	*Senilis.*
Corrugata.	*Cylindrica cristata.*	*Diademata.*
Amyclæa.	*Microdasys.*	

Opuntias are easily grown, and propagate very

freely. *O. Rafinesquina* and *O. humilis* are hardy in the southern counties. They should be planted on a rockwork or other dry situation. I find they do not like London smoke, and of course damp will not agree with them anywhere.

Of EPIPHYLLUMS and PHYLLOCACTUS I think I need say nothing, as they are generally known as greenhouse flowering plants, excepting that I often see the two confounded. If looked into, it will be seen at once that Epiphyllum has its flowers at the apex of a jointed stem or branch, while Phyllocactus produces larger flowers, which are regular, and trumpet shaped on the margins of the stems. The Phyllocactuses are more hardy than Epiphyllums, and require to be kept dry during winter if expected to flower freely.

RHIPSALIS.—Before leaving this great order I must mention the Rhipsalis. This is a genus of small flowering Cacti that require stove treatment. It is exceedingly variable. The following are very curious plants, and scarcely handsome.

RHIPSALIS.

Funalis.	*Saglionis.*	*Rhombea.*
Mesembryanthoides.	*Salicornoides.*	*Paradoxa.*

An exceedingly curious Cactus is found in the solitary *Pelicophora ascelliformis*, a most rare and abnormal object, reminding one of the geological specimens of *Cyphosoma texanum* rather than a living plant.

LEUCHTENBERGIA is another of the missing links between a porcupine and a cactus, its spines having a horny texture, and growing six to ten inches long. The plant is of Mexican origin, and grows very slowly in the same temperature as other Cacti.

ANHALONIUM is another of the fossil-formed stragglers in this decade of the world's existence. Whether some of these fellows have managed to get through the ages of change when their brothers succumbed, I know not ; but it is evident by the slow way they have of growing and reproducing themselves, that they got their ideas before the modern Yankee was about, or steam travelling was invented.

ANHALONIUM.

Elongatum.   *Prysmaticum.*   *Salzatum.*

The above are the only known species, though catalogues have more names.

PILOCEREUS is the "Old Man Cactus," *par excellence*, but the characters of the genus are not generally understood, and the species are commonly confounded with those of Cereus. The prevalence of white-haired species amongst the genera of cactaceous plants renders the specific designation "senilis" almost too common, and it becomes a question at last, which is the genuine old Simon who is to be known by his hoary locks? A very striking Old Man sort in this class is *Pilocereus Dautwitzi*, and a good companion in another line is *Mamillaria senilis*.

It is worthy of remark that Pilocereus differs from Cereus in the flowers coming from the apex, whereas in Cereus they are lateral, the tube of the flower is shorter, and the plants are more or less hirsute, especially on the top; in fact, they have quite an aristocratic appearance. They are not fast growers, and during winter must be quite dry. This genus is spared by scale, thrips, and bugs, for these pests never touch the plants; at all events I never saw one on a Pilocereus yet.

PILOCEREUS.

Senilis.	*Jubatus.*	*Hoppenstedti.*
Dautwitzi.	*Glaucescens.*	*Peacockii.*
Millitari.	*Celsiana.*	

These are all distinct and beautiful species. I have seen plants that parties have kept for years, and only gave them water three or four times during the season, but they only exist; such meagre management does not answer.

ECHINOCEREUS is a small genus of prostrate plants with flowers excelling in size and beauty, in comparison with their stature, all the others. They mostly come from the far north of California, and are easily grown. The best are

ECHINOCEREUS.

Blanki.	*Cinerascens.*	*Stramineus.*
Procumbens.	*Pectiniferus.*	*Leeanus.*
Polyacanthus.	*Pectiniferus amœna.*	*Roemeni.*

GRAFTING CACTI.

This is a process whereby slow growers may be got on faster, and many curious and fanciful objects may be made by those who have a fancy that way.

The plan is to cut the scion, and stock equally flat with a sharp knife, and bring some part of the centre of each growth in connection, then tie the two firmly with strong worsted, so that they are kept pressed and immovable. It is often best to put three sticks to steady the graft. May and June are the best months for the purpose. The stock should be selected according to the vigour of the scion. For large growing kinds *Cereus peruvianus* answers well ; for smaller kinds *C. tortuosus* is preferable. These are hardier and more constant in their growth than many other free-growing sorts that might be chosen. If a tenderer stock than the scion is used, the result is often that after a season the stock goes off, and starves its employer—a sort of strike. They should be left tied for six or eight weeks, when the worsted may be cut carefully—in truth Cacti are more easily grafted than other plants in the vegetable kingdom.

INSECT PESTS.

Mr. Croucher has favoured us with the following, which has been specially written for this work :—

" ' All these things are against me,' is often the cry of plant amateurs, when they go to inspect their pets, and find some of those omnivorous creatures of the animal world making a delicious meal of the tenderest and most important part of a special plant; for be it known unto all men, and women whom it may concern, that these creatures are epicureans, in most cases. Therefore, seeing they have no respect for our favourites, we adopt the only alternative, and go in for exterminating them, in spite of the game laws.

"The greatest pest to succulents is the *red spider*. This may be kept under by keeping the air moderately dry and cool; if they get about it it is a sure sign that the temperature is too high; should they unfortunately get the mastery, set the particular plant out in the open air.

"The next is mealey bug; they may be killed by fumigating or by hand; if there are but few the latter will be best; green fly get on plants mostly in the spring, but they are easily got rid of by fumigating or syringing, but the plant should be put into the open air to syringe, or the rascals get up again.

"The brown scale is a great pest, and can only be got rid of by hand-picking; this should be done carefully, as the young ones are so minute that they may escape, and then they will start, on their own account, a new colony.

"Soap and water, Gishurst compound, and those sorts of mixtures are often recommended, but they generally end with the destruction of the plant. In using tobacco it will greatly add to the effect, and save material, if a water-proof bag be put over the plant or plants to keep the fumes in ; and then it can be done in the open garden, which will prevent the disagreeable smell in the house or case ; after fumigating, the next morning the plants should be well syringed.

" There is a form of mealey bug which gets on the roots of some Cacti at times; whenever these are discovered, it is best to shake all the soil off the roots, and thoroughly wash them in clean water, using a clean pot, and by no means using the old pot until it has been well scrubed.

" It is well to keep a small brush, and a long pin or spine at hand, so that whenever an enemy is detected, it is easy to slay him at once, and as Cowper said of the snake, 'teach him never to come there no more.'

" The plants most generally affected by scale, and mealey bugs, are Mammillaria, and though I have not examined any of these creatures phrenologically, I have reason to believe they have large secretiveness, generally getting in the most out of the way places, so a constant watch must be kept in these spots, or a colony will get a good footing before detected."

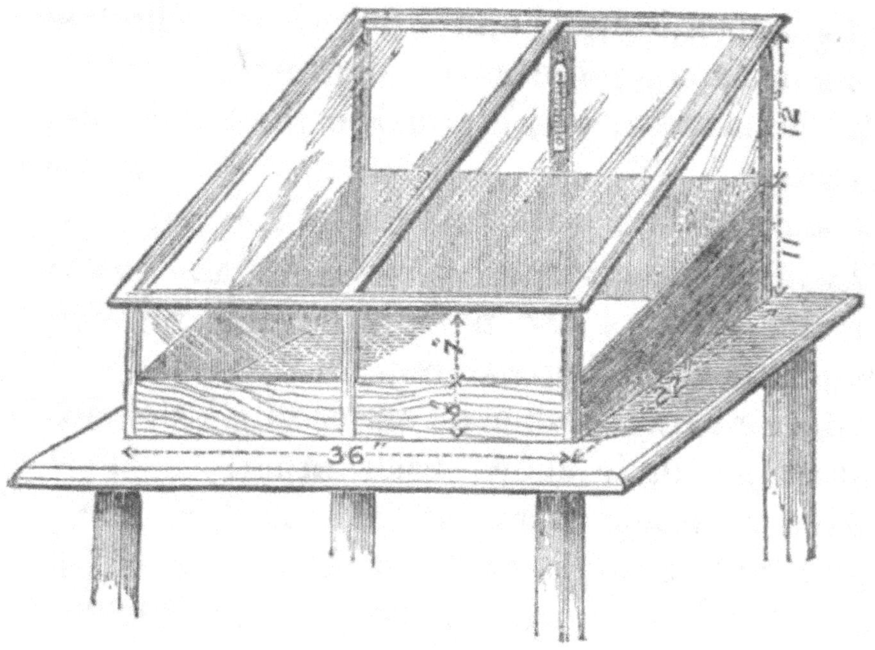

Fig. 17.

THE MINIATURE GREENHOUSE.

It is now time to speak of our own proceedings on the subject. We constructed a case or miniature greenhouse to stand on a table in our room before the window.   It is three feet long and twenty-two inches wide, with sides of deal part of the way up, the upper part being glass; the back is twenty-four inches high, viz., eleven inches of wood below and thirteen inches of glass in the upper part.   The front of the greenhouse is twelve inches high, viz. five inches of wood and seven of glass; the slanting lid is also glass.

The sides are made of deal and glass in the same proportion as the back and front.   The sides might

G

be constructed entirely of glass, but they would be liable to be broken by the pots. Our case is made so that the pots are all slightly below the top of the wooden sides.

The case has a deal bottom, on which a zinc tray is fitted inside for the purpose of catching any water that may run through the pots, or overflow them when the plants are being watered.

Above the zinc tray there are a series of six shelves rising about an inch above each other. These shelves give standing room for fifty-four little pots (about four inches high) of *Cacti* and other small succulents. The pots are numbered, the figures being stamped on small pieces of zinc, which are partly thrust into the mould of each pot, and the names of the several plants are given on a cardboard. [The zinc number is seen in the pot of plant No. 31, page 98.] To bring the tops of the pots to about the same level we placed small blocks of wood under such pots as were too low.

The top or lid of the case is like a picture-frame on hinges, which permits its being taken off in the summer months or at other times, and there are supports which can be turned up on each side of the case to sustain the lid four inches or twelve inches high to ventilate the plants. With care, the whole greenhouse (full of plants) may be easily turned round on the table by one person, according as the back or front is required to face the sun.

Our window has a westerly aspect.

Furthermore, the front is so constructed that the glass can be drawn out to enable a person to move the pots which are in front more conveniently than by reaching them from above. It would be an improvement to make the front with two pieces of glass —one to slide over the other similar to a sash. No part would then project beyond the side of the case when part of the front was opened.

As it would be inconvenient to water such small and delicate plants with a common water pot, we use a piece of bent gas piping for the purpose; it is about twelve inches long, and has a small funnel at the top. Water from a jug can thus be conveyed direct to any particular plant without the risk of injuring others.

We experienced much difficulty in knowing when the plants required watering. Some gardeners adopt the plan of tapping the outside of the pot. When the earth within is saturated, the sound is similar to that of a solid body; but when the soil is not saturated, the sound is more hollow, from the interstices of the mould being filled with air instead of water. The difference will best be understood by tapping against the side of the pot immediately after watering, and against the same when dry. Others judge by the weight of a pot whether the plant requires watering. It is well to take out all the pots occasionally, and then the state of the mould can be more easily ascertained. They could also be syringed better out of the case than in it. We occasionally in the summer take all the pots out of the case, and place them in a large flat iron or zinc tray, and give them a good drenching from a water-pot having a fine rose attached to it. Such watering is of great benefit to the plants.

The case is painted within and without a mahogany colour, and it is ornamented to some extent by having a gold beading or moulding placed along the top edging of the wooden sides, and also on the uprights—all outside. A mahogany case would look far better, especially if the case was kept in a sitting-room, but it would be much more expensive. Ours, just as it has been described, cost about twelve shillings; we did the carpenter's work. In fact, the case itself originally only cost one shilling; it had been a packing case from a chemist, and we cut it down somewhat to the form of a desk. At the back of the case inside a thermometer is suspended. We shall speak of the temperature in page 126. It would not be difficult to have a zinc tray at the bottom, which might be filled with hot water twice a day during very severe cold in the winter, with a pipe opening outside to allow of the escape of steam; but the case would have to be made deeper to admit such. [See Miss Maling's plan, page 127.]

We now give a list of our plants; those too large for the miniature greenhouse have an asterisk to the number, thus: *16, *Opuntia Rafinesquiana.*

CACTI, &c., &c., IN THE CASE, NOVEMBER, 1876.

No.	Name.	Native habitat.
1	Echinopsis multiplex ...	Brazil
2	Cereus strigosus	Chili
3	Cereus Peruvianus	Peru
4	Mamillaria gracilis	Mexico
5	Cotyledon pulverulenta ...	S. Africa
6	Crassula lycopodioides ...	The Cape of Good Hope
7	Mamillaria discolor	S. America
8	Phillocactus Jenkinsoni ...	Hybrid
9	Opuntia cylindrica	West Indies
10	Mesembryanthemum densum	Africa
11	Sempervivum Haworthii ...	Canary Islands
12	Aloe distans	S. Africa
13	Euphorbia imbricata... ...	S. Africa
14	Opuntia Kleinii	Mexico
15	Cereus Napoleonis	West Indies
*16	Opuntia Rafinesquiana ...	S. America
17	Rochea (Crassula) falcata ...	The Cape
18	Kleinia articulata	The Cape
*19	Mesem. echinatum	The Cape
20	Echinopsis Eyriesii	Mexico
21	Echinopsis Zuccariniana rosea	S. America
22	Gasteria verrucosa	The Cape
*23	Sempervivum arboreum ...	Levant
24	Epiphyllum truncatum ...	Brazil
25	Echinocactus Ottonis ...	Mexico
26	Haworthia cuspidata ...	The Cape
*27	Cereus flagelliformis ...	Peru
28	Haworthia attenuata ...	The Cape
*29	Opuntia elatior	West Indies
30	Aloe prolifera...	Africa
31	Aloe variegata	The Cape
*32	Crassula quadrifida	The Cape
33	Cereus serpentinus	Mexico
34	Same as No. 1	
35	Pachyphytum bracteosum ...	Mexico

CACTI, &C., &C., IN THE CASE, NOVEMBER, 1876

CACTI, &C., &C., IN THE CASE, NOVEMBER, 1876
(Continued).

No.	Name.	Native habitat.
36	Phyllocactus Jenkinsoni ...	Hybrid
37	Mamillaria stella aurata ...	S. America
38	Gasteria marmorata	The Cape
39	Opuntia exuviata	S. America
*40	Opuntia decumana	S. America
41	Crassula arborescens... ...	S. Africa
42	Crassula portulacea	S. Africa
*43	Aloe fructicosa	The Cape
44	Same as No. 22	
45	Mamillaria stellaris	S. America
46	Agave Americana	S. America
47	Opuntia microdasys	Trop. America
48	Stapelia humilis	Africa
*49	Cactus speciosa elegans ...	S. America
50	Mamillaria longimamma ...	West Indies
51	Semper. arachnoideum ...	S. Europe
52	Same as No. 49	
*53	Cereus Mallissoni	Hybrid
54	Opuntia ovata	S. America
55	Cereus candicans	Mexico
56	Echinocactus gibbosus ...	West Indies
57	Stapelia radiata	The Cape
58	Cotyledon Cooperi	The Cape
59	Same as No. 25	
*60	Aloe africana...	Africa
61	Pachyphytum roseum ...	Mexico
62	Opuntia brasiliensis	Brazil
63	Opuntia cylindrica cristata...	America
64	Mesem. tigrinum	Africa
65	Mamillaria Wildiana ...	West Indies

We find Mesembryanthemums are most difficult to keep
during the winter. We cannot resist the temptation to water
them and this is apt to kill them, but if so it will only cost
from 4d. to 6d. each to replace them in the spring.

DESCRIPTION OF THE CACTI, &c.

(The numerical order cannot be exactly observed in consequence of the size of the Figures or Cuts.)

1. *Echinopsis multiplex.*—This dark green, globular *Cactus* is about four inches high and two and a half inches in diameter towards the top, of the shape of a large inverted pear. It is named from its being prickly, and of many ribs, angles, or turnings. There are thirteen perpendicular angular ribs or belts, on the edges of which tufts of spines grow at regular intervals. These are most accurately placed, not opposite to those on the adjoining rib, but intermediately. The spines appear as stars opposite each each other on alternate ribs; thus affording more space for their growth. It has seven young plants projecting from its side, and the flower of this *Cactus* is rosy pink.

2. *Cereus strigosus,* a cylindrical plant with many more ribs, considering its diameter, than the *Echinopsis multiplex.* It is lean or lank, as its name implies; it has sixteen ribs or angles in a diameter of one-and-half inches, and they are not so deeply indented. The spines are close, and interlace each other in every direction.

5. *Cotyledon pulverulenta* has a stiff and formal appearance; it is a slender plant, with but a few strong flat leaves like the blade of a paddle. These are dusted with greyish white; hence its name *pulverulenta.* *Cotyledon* is derived from a Greek word signifying a vessel or cup; the leaves of many of these plants are of this form.

Fig. 18, CEREUS PERUVIANUS.

3. *Cereus Peruvianus.*—A dark green color, five inches high ; growing like a truncated cone, with six large deep ribs of three-quarters of an inch in depth. We counted eighteen clusters of spines on the edge of one rib from base to crown. We hear that it will grow twenty feet in height.

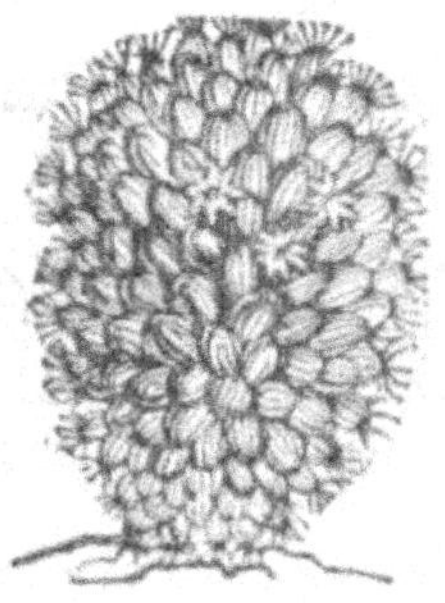

Fig. 19, MAMILLARIA GRACILIS.

4. *Mamillaria gracilis.*—A plant more cylindrical than No. 1, and much smaller. It has no ribs, but is covered with slender protuberances (literally teats or paps, as its name denotes) ; each is termi-nated with a tuft of spines. This plant is very prolific, for fourteen young ones were thrust out from its sides last year ; in fact, it appears always projecting young plants, and one of these in its turn has five little infants perched on its youthful head

We have made a special stone pot of Portland cement for this interesting *Mamillaria ;* the pot is of irregular shape, about three inches deep and nine inches long. It now contains the parent plant, and seven of its first offspring growing around it, with a tolerable family of grandchildren. The fruit of the *Mamillaria* is of a red colour, and has the flavour of fried beef !

6. *Crassula lycopodioides.*—This is an interesting dark green plant somewhat like stone crop, but the branches are three or four inches long, with four rows of close-set minute leaves disposed in regular lines, like the seed of the common English plaintain. It has about seventy stems rising up; for, although some of the branches fall down over the side of the pot, the terminations all grow upwards, like green serrated pipes. The extreme tops are of a lighter green, which gives it a pretty appearance.

7. *Mamillaria discolor* has the peculiar exterior of the *Mamillaria gracilis*; but it is much larger, being about four inches high and two and a half inches in diameter. The protuberances are so close together that they are almost hidden by the multitude of spines. *Discolor* signifies sundry colours or tints. It looks green 'or grey as the spines predominate or otherwise. Two young plants are growing on its side.

9. *Opuntia cylindrica.*—This *Opuntia* is of a totally different form to that of the generality of plants of this genus. Instead of being ovate and flattened like the sole of a shoe, it is cylindrical. It is seven.

inches high, and nearly an inch in diameter. There are what resemble a series of soft green thorns or small tongues (rather curved) standing a quarter of an inch asunder in regular lines on the sides and top of the cylinder. These soft thorns or leaves in course of time shrivel up, and are succeeded by the spines, which are in our plant of great delicacy, standing out like minute silver needles or hairs.

Fig. 20, PHILLOCACTUS JENKINSONI.

8. *Phillocactus Jenkinsoni* is a hybrid plant. It has upright, stiff, flat leaves, but the shoots from the leaves are eccentric—some are triangular, and others are almost globular—but all with spines on the edges. The flowers are very beautiful. See the description of succulents in the Royal Gardens at Kew, page 44.

11. *Sempervivum Haworthii.* — This plant has a rosette of small stout leaves like the House-leek, but more compressed, growing on the termination of its branches. On this plant there are twelve of these rosettes. [See Fig. 55, page 124.]

10. *Mesembryanthemum densum* is much admired. It grows in clusters of little solid cylindrical light green leaves, about half an inch long. The top of each terminates with a star of minute spines or hairs. The small solid leaves appear glistening or frosted, rather similar to some of the ice plants.

12. *Aloe distans* appears like an overgrown Aloe, as though running to seed. The leaves are placed far asunder on the stalk, and their edges have sharp prickles standing out resembling small white teeth.

13. *Euphorbia imbricata.* — This African plant is dark green ; about four inches high ; in shape some-what like a cone. It has nine ribs or angles run-ning rather irregularly from the base to the top, like ridged tiles (hence its name), with strong spikes at various distances on the ridges, giving it a quaint appearance. A young plant about a quarter of an inch long is jutting out from one side. Mr. Shirley Hibberd remarks that the spiny species of the *Euphorbia* may sometimes be confounded with the *Cactus* family ; but in the former the spines are gene-rally produced singly, whereas in the *Cactus* the spines are in clusters or tufts.

14. *Opuntia Kleinii*, we believe, is commonly known as stags' horns, as it grows very irregularly. It has slender cylindrical branches, with tufts of spines covering it. This plant shrivelled up so much in the spring that we supposed it was dead. How-ever, on taking it up, and cleansing the roots, and

repotting it in fresh soil, it revived wonderfully, and has pushed out two vigorous shoots. We should not be too ready to imagine that these plants are dead, they have astonishing vitality.

Fig. 21, CEREUS NAPOLEONIS.

15. *Cereus Napoleonis.*—This grows similar to a slender, tapering, upright rod. It was five inches high last November, and in a year it has grown about six inches, being now about eleven inches in height. It has six rows of spines from its apex to the base; the clusters of spines are placed alternately, as in No. 1, the *Echinopsis multiplex.*

16. *Opuntia Rafinesquiana.*—We have only quite lately had this given to us. It is in a very shrivelled state, and therefore we are not able to speak of it more fully. The joints are rounder and not so long as the *Opuntia elatior.* We believe it has been recommended as a bedding plant.

17. *Rochea* (or *Crassula*) *falcata* is a singular growing plant. The greyish leaves are of a curious shape, somewhat similar to the blade of a short scythe; hence its name *falcata*. These blades or lobes turn first to the right and then to the left; they may also be compared to the segment of a circle. Our plant has two leaves to the right hand and two to the left, with two in the middle just parting for good. Its bloom is orange scarlet, very bright, and continues a long time in flower; a charming plant.

18. *Kleinia articulata.*—This plant has no pretensions to beauty, but has a tube-like appearance, of a light green colour, and is commonly called the candle plant. The tube or stem does not taper like the *Cereus Napoleonis* (No. 15), neither has it any ridges or spines. It throws out a few straggling branches, with irregular-shaped leaves, from its top and sides. These, if taken off and planted, will soon take root. Articulata signifies jointed. The tube or stem of the plant appears at intervals as if tied in or almost divided into lengths.

19. *Mesembryanthemum echinatum* has the appearance of a miniature tree. The leaves are of odd shape—in fact, the plant is thickly studded with small gherkins or green pods; it is one of the ice plants. The pods shine as though covered with frost, and has numerous soft prickles issuing from them like the chesnut. The flower is similar to a minute white daisy.

22. *Gasteria verrucosa.*—Commonly known as the adder's tongue from the shape and spotted state of the leaves, which do not spread out on every side as other plants, but grow down on each other like the narrow leaves of a small book—they are speckled with white minute warts, hence its name *verrucosa.* The *Gasterias* are classed with Aloes.

Fig. 22.— ECHINOPSIS EYRIESII.

20. *Echinopsis Eyriesii* is more globular than the *Echinopsis multiplex* (No. 1): the thirteen ribs or angles are more indented, and the spines are not so long—it is an inch and three quarters high, and an inch and a half in diameter; the seats of the spines appear as little white tufts, which adds to its appearance.

23. *Sempervivum arboreum.*—A tall growing variety of No. 11. [See Fig. 53, page 122.]

24. *Epiphyllum truncatum.*—A drooping plant—the flat leaves appear maimed—mangled or disjointed ; the flowers of this succulent are a rose pink. We have seen and greatly admired them in conservatories in full bloom from December to April—they somewhat resemble a beautiful fuchsia.

25. *Echinocactus Ottonis.*—This is melon shaped, with only eleven ribs or angles, though the mere number of these does not indicate any peculiarity, for the number of ribs, we are informed, is capricious. It is a very free flowering plant, even in its small state.

Fig. 23, ECHINOPSIS ZUCCARINIANA.

21. *Echinopsis Zuccariniana rosea.*—This Cactus is globular and very compact, more the form of a melon—the ribs are decided and very angular.

26. *Haworthia cuspidata.*—Plants having this prefix are named after Haworth, the botanist; it is somewhat of the Houseleek character, but the leaves

are exceedingly solid, about half an inch thick, of a bluish white colour, semi-transparent like ground glass.

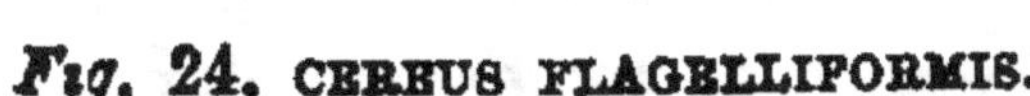

Fig. 24, CEREUS FLAGELLIFORMIS.

27. *Cereus flagelliformis.*—This, we believe, is commonly known as the creeping cereus or rat-tail Cereus; it has the appearance of a knot of slender drooping tails, thickly covered with small spines—the plant should be suspended, as it will trail down three or four feet. The flowers stand out direct from the slender shoots and are of a beautiful pink colour. They can frequently be met with in Covent Garden Market at 1s. each. [See page 13.]

28. *Haworthia attenuata.*—This is a pretty plant somewhat like the Aloe in its habit of growth. The thick stout leaves are more angular and pointed. They are beautifully spotted underneath—the under-part has the appearance of being studded with small white pearls. This is, we think, the plant referred to by Mr. Bradley in page 9.

30. *Aloe prolifera,* rather similar to the *Aloe dis tans* (No. 12) but dwarf in its nature—it has prickles on the edges of its leaves.

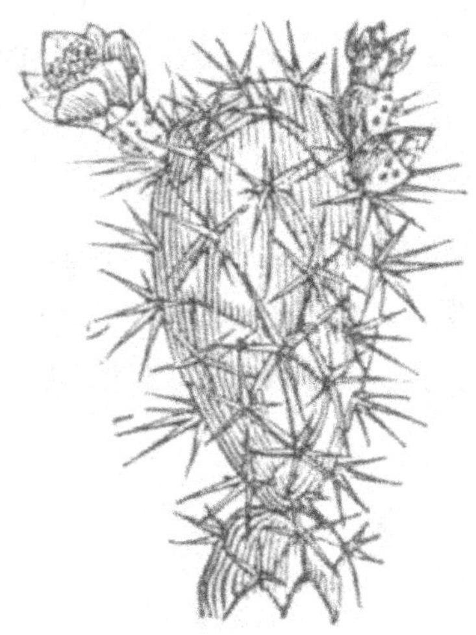

Fig. 25.—OPUNTIA ELATIOR,

So named by Loudon, but it is to be considered the *O. polyanthus.* Our plant has scarcely any spines, and in this respect is unlike the above drawing.

29. *Opuntia elatior.*—This latter word signifies lofty, as the habit of this *Opuntia* is to mount upwards. We had two leaves given to us joined together like the figure **8** only more elliptical. We planted it in a pot the height being seven inches; it soon made three shoots from the top, but one grew so vigorously that the other two made no further effort— the one shoot which grows crossways on that below attained the height of six inches in about three months—on each side of this flat ovate leaf ard like the sole of a shoe, small soft green thorns shot out slightly curved as in No. 9 ; these in course of time withered and fell off, and the spines appeared. Further remarks respecting the *Opuntia* have been given in other pages. Some of the Opuntias grow

H

a considerable height, we observed them at the
Royal Garden, Kew, about ten or twelve feet high ;
in these instances the sole and ovate form of the
thick lower joint gradually disappears or is
developed into a stem of woody fibre almost cylindrical—if this did not occur the ponderous weight
of the plant above could not be supported.

Fig. 26.—ALOE VARIEGATA.
Drawn by Mr. Rogers from our plant.

3**1**. *Aloe variegata*, one of the prettiest plants we
possess. It is of a most decided character—the
thick strong green leaves stand up like pointed
horns or swords, and are beautifully mottled, or
rather have bands or bars of white across them
sometimes termed partridge breast. This Aloe is of
remarkably slow growth : ours is about six inches
high and probably is eight years old—it has seven-

teen stiff pointed mottled leaves slightly curved outwards towards their tops. Every collection of succulents should include this beautiful Aloe; our plant
has three young offsets springing from its root as is
the case with Aloes and Agaves.

32. *Crassula quadrifides* is an uninteresting plant—
we may add, not worth keeping. It has thick rounded
leaves of a dull brownish green colour. Perhaps we
should not write disparagingly of this plant, for like
many plain people it may possess great qualifications
although unknown to us.

33. *Cereus serpentinus.*—Our plant is about seven
inches high of the form of a cucumber, with eleven
ribs or angles running up its stem. On the edges
of these ribs as usual the bunches of spines are
formed. A plant of this species at the Crystal
Palace is about eight feet high.

34. Same as No. 1.

35. *Pachyphytum bracteosum.*—This is a singular
plant with solid greenish leaves dusted with white,
in shape like an almond. At Kew Gardens these
white powdered plants are generally kept covered in
glass cases, we suppose to prevent parties touching
them, for the white powder comes off on the hand.
They have the appearance of frosted silver.

36. Same as No. 8.

38. *Gasteria marmorata.*—Similar in form to
Gasteria verrucosa, but the leaves are light green and
are not so rough—their color much resemble varie-
gated green marble.

Fig. 27.—MAMILLARIA STELLA AURATA

According to Loudon, this figure represents *Mamillaria tenuis*, but it resembles our plant.

37. *Mamillaria stella aurata.*—Very similar to *Mamillaria gracilis*, but it has a golden hue.

39. *Opuntia exuviata.*—This *Opuntia* is totally unlike *O. elatior* (No. 29)—the sole of the shoe is absent — neither does it resemble the *Opuntia cylindrica* (No. 9), but is rather similar to the *Opuntia Kleinii* (No. 14). The stem is knotty or indented and the spines are disposed irregularly on it—it is a series of long protuberances. *Exuviata* signifies the cast skin of a snake, shrivelled up.

40. *Opuntia decumana.*—A name indicative of great size, and well it may be termed such ; for while a joint or blade of the *Opuntia elatior* (No. 29) is two inches wide, the *decumana* is five inches in width and eight inches high. This plant was given to us by a friend who purchased it in the market at Antwerp— it is of singular appearance and has six large leaves growing on the top and sides of the parent joint ;

Fig. 28.—OPUNTIA DECUMANA.

one of these leaves is ten inches high and three
inches broad—two of the leaves are nearly circular
and the other three nine inches high—the leaves have
spines on each side at regular intervals. We made
the above rough sketch of our plant to a scale of
one-eighth of an inch to one inch. It truly is the
Goliath of the collection.

41. *Crassula arborescens.*—The leaves are ovate
(egg) shaped and thick, rather curved, and of light
green colour minutely spotted—also slightly edged
with crimson; large plants can be seen at Kew grown
into thick stunted trees of most ancient appearance.

The word *Crassula* is taken from crassus, thick—in allusion to the fleshy nature of the leaves of all the species.

42. *Crassula portulacea.*—This plant is of the same character as the preceding, but the leaves are smaller and not edged with crimson—it is dark green. We have seen a perfect little tree of this *Crassula* in a window near us—the branches are woody and would give one the idea of a quaint liliputian tree. We have also noticed a specimen at Kew about four feet high which has its stem as thick as one's arm, at least four inches in diameter.

43. *Aloe fructicosa.*—This *Aloe* may frequently be seen in windows and conservatories. Of tall growth. it is of light pale green colour; the leaves are very much curved downwards, narrow, and strongly serrated on the edges.

44. Same as No. 22.

Fig. 29.—MAMILLARIA STELLARIS.

45. *Mamillaria stellaris* is most interesting, it is very dwarf, as if squatting on the earth in the pot, and spreading itself out, with its five young ones round it. The spines are numerous and silvery-

looking ; it appears at a little distance like a large cobweb plant. (See Fig. 31, p. 107.) *Stellaris* signifies a star.

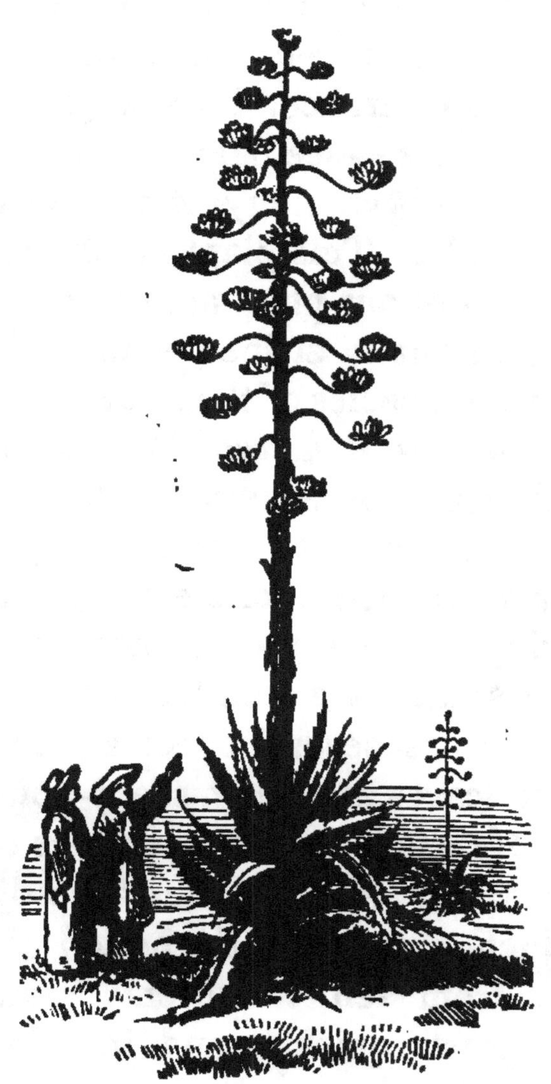

Fig. 30.—AGAVE AMERICANA.

46. *Agave Americana.*—A noble plant, in fact the king of succulents. We cannot be content to give it a brief notice, but must enter more fully on its

description. It is well known that the *Agave* adorns almost every conservatory, and is seen in vases and on lawns or terraces in the summer season. The word *Agave* is derived from the Greek, signifying admirable, which this genus of succulents truly is, considering its appearance, its size (one leaf sometimes weighs 12 lbs.—see page 47), and the variety of its flowers. In Mythology, *Agave* is the name of one of the Nereids. This plant much resembles the Aloe—the leaves of our plant are edged with yellow, others are occasionally striped with white and red. There are several species of the *Agave.* This plant is sometimes called the *American Aloe;* but the Aloe is a native of Africa, not America. We take the following from " Ripley's New American Cyclopædia " : —" The *Agave* produces a circle of stiff erect fleshy leaves, growing on the top of a short woody trunk, bearing flowers in a long terminal woody spire. Of this plant there are several species. In the *Agave Americana* the leaves are spiny, sharp-pointed, bluish green, each of which leaves continues to exist for many years. The *Agave* varies according to the region in which it grows, in the period of its coming to maturity, from ten to seventy years. In hot countries it grows quickly, and in colder climates much slower. So soon as it arrives at its maturity it sends forth a stem forty feet in height, which puts out numerous branches, forming a cylindrical pyramid of perfect symmetry, each crowned with a cluster of greenish yellow flowers, which continue in perfect bloom during a period of several months in succession. From the intertropical region of America it has been transported to almost every temperate region. In England, the United States, and France, it is a tender greenhouse plant ; but in Spain, Italy, Sicily, and the Barbary States, it is perfectly naturalised, and gives to those beautiful countries a picture of tropical vegetation mingled with the foliage and scenery of temperate Europe. About Milan and other towns in Lombardy, where it will not endure the winter, they use imitations of copper,* so well formed and painted as to be readily mistaken for the original. A fermented liquor is made from the *Agave* sap, and is much esteemed by the Mexicans. A coarse thread is made from the fibres of the leaves, from which the ancient Mexicans made paper. The dried flower stems constitute a thatch impervious to the weather. Soap is made from an extract of the leaves, which lathers in salt water as well as in fresh, and from the centre of the stem, split longitudinally, a substitute is obtained for a hone or razor strop, which, owing to the particles of silica which forms one of its constituents, has the property of speedily bringing steel to a fine edge. It is also used as a substitute for cork. The *Agave*, no sooner has it flowered—at whatever period of its existence that may occur—than it at once withers and dies. We have a small *Agave* in our case, and a larger one in the room with three offsets in the pot.

---

* We have seen these in London.

47. *Opuntia microdasys* is a pretty plant. Ours has two stiff light green leaves standing up on the parent stem like a flattened spoon, studded with small tufts of minute spines, similar to a pincushion—hence its name; since the spring each of these two leaves has produced two other leaves, the counterpart of those below which sit on the parent leaf, so now the plant has seven leaves. They remind one of athletic performers standing one above another.

48. *Stapelia humilis.*—This much resembles the *Stapelia radiata*, No. 57 (which we shall describe presently), but the light green shoots, for we cannot call them leaves, are more slender and not so obtuse as the *radiata*. *Humilis* signifies weak or poor.

49. *Phyllocactus speciosa elegans* is frequently seen in windows, but with the tops sadly broken off and damaged. The leaves are one long narrow strip of green, indented on the edges, like some sea weed; but, strange to say, the leaves on one and the same plant differ in form; some are three sided, some quite flat, and others again four sided; the section of these latter, if cut asunder, would be a cross thus +, and there are also little shoots, almost globular. The centre leaf of our plant is fourteen inches high by an inch and a half wide. This is three sided, and doubtless it is thus much strengthened by this formation, for the long narrow leaf could not stand up at all if a mere shread like a piece of narrow ribbon. These four and three-sided leaves remind one forcibly

of the construction of iron girders and columns.
that are now so extensively employed in buildings.
The flowers are a beautiful pink colour, and
they are produced direct from the sides of the
leaves. Ours had three blossoms, nearly the
size of a tea cup, in shape like a lily, and
honey exuded from them in large drops. We have
seen fine plants in flower at Covent Garden for 2s.
each; it is easily propagated. A piece of a leaf,
after being allowed to dry for a week, has only to be
put into sandy loam, when it will soon grow.

50. *Mamillaria longimamma* resembles a cluster of
green cones, jutting out in every direction from a
centre. Our plant has eighteen of these protuberances; the top of each has a tuft of long spines or
bristles, nine in number.

Fig. 31.—SEMPERVIVUM ARACHNOIDEUM

51. *Sempervivum arachnoideum*—the cobweb plant
—is dwarf, very much smaller than the House-leek,
and covered with white fibres, crossing back-

wards and forwards from leaf to leaf as though a spider had spun its web amongst and over the plants; it grows in clusters, similar to the House-leek. Flower rose colour.

52. Same as No. 49.

53. *Cereus Mallissoni.*—This is a trailing plant, rather similar to the *Cereus flagelliformis* (No. 27), a cluster of slender tails, falling over the side of the pot, but the ridges and rows of spines are not so numerous; the shoots are larger or coarser than No. 27. One shoot stands erect fourteen inches, and another nearly as high. We are anxious to know when it intends to be amenable to the laws of its nature, and turn down like the other members of its family. It is dangerous even for a plant to be so aspiring, for one evening, in drawing down the blind, the top of the longest shoot was broken off, for the plant, being far too large to be kept in the case, was standing, with others, on a shelf before our room window. The piece broken off was put into a pot and is now thriving; two shoots have been produced where the top was broken off. Thus an accident of this kind eventually tends to increase the stock of succulents, as you are enabled to exchange these duplicate plants for other kinds you may not possess.

54. *Opuntia ovata.*—Another strange specimen of the Opuntia family. Instead of being one uniform cylinder as *O. cylindrica*, No. 9, or as a knotty stem like *O. exuviata*, No. 39, this plant assumes the egg

form, rather elongated, covered with clusters of spines. From the parent stem our small plant has five of these stumpy shoots of an inch long, and on one of them sits another little protuberance; doubtless, next season, if it lives through the winter each of the other four protuberances will thrust out another family.

55. *Cereus candicans.*—This much resembles the *Echinopsis multiplex;* it has ten ridges, and the spines are very large and thick set. *Candicans* is the Latin for whitish. It is marked with white splotches, whether it will be more so than at present time will prove.

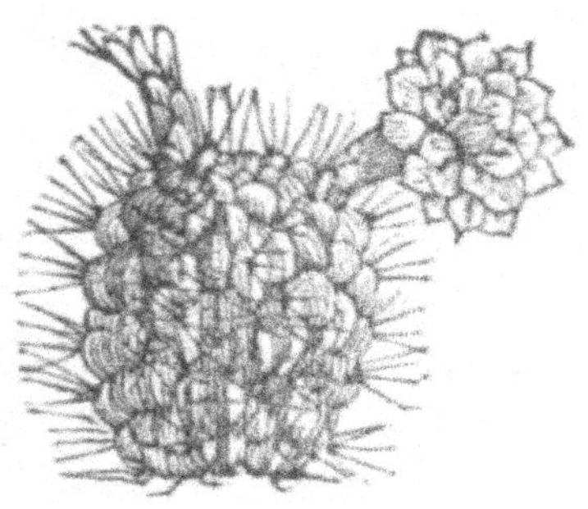

Fig. 32.—ECHINOCACTUS GIBBOSUS.

56. *Echinocactus gibbosus* (protuberant).—A small spherical cactus with numerous bumps or swellings; from the centre of each, eight spines project. Its name implies bunched or bossed.

58. *Cotyledon Cooperi* has numerous small dark green solid leaves—lozenge-shaped growing in clusters from no apparent stem. If a leaf falls off,

in a short time it throws out roots and will soon establish itself as a distinct plant.

59. Same as No. 25.

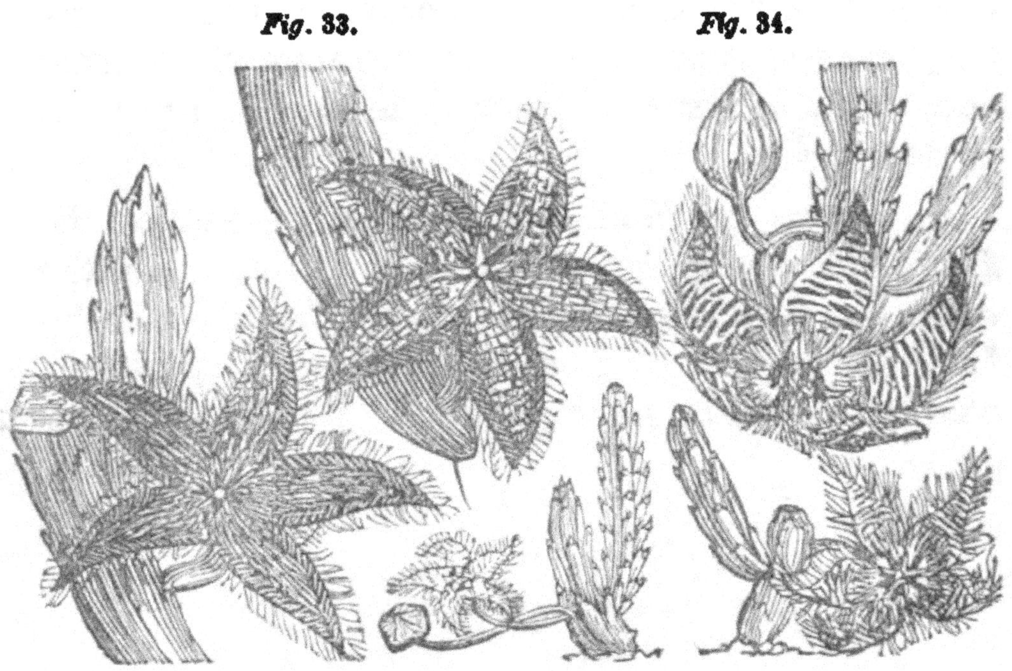

Fig. 33.   Fig. 34.

Fig. 35.   Fig. 36.   Fig. 37.

Fig. 33, STAPELIA AMBIGUA. *Fig.* 34, S. ARTRA. *Fig.* 35, S. GRANDIFLORA. *Fig* 36, S. RUFA. *Fig.* 37, S. NAMATA.

We could not find in Loudon the Stapelias we have as Nos. 48 and 57, but as the flowers are all of the same character we give the above five species.

57. *Stapelia radiata.*—A singular looking plant, somewhat resembling a cluster of small cucumbers from half an inch to an inch long, growing in different directions, covered with small scaly protuberances instead of spines. The word *radiata* signifies set about with spokes—radiating. Linnæus named the plant Stapelia in memory of an eminent

physician of Amsterdam. This is one of the Carrion flowers of South Africa, and is leafless like other succulents; of diminutive stem, it is usually four cornered, and the curiously blotched large flowers resemble small star-fish; these emit a nauseous odour which is so attractive to flies that they deposit their eggs upon them in great numbers in their native country. When such are brought to life by the heat of the sun, they find nothing to sustain them and thus quickly die. There are numerous species of this plant in Africa, and some are used as articles of food by the Hottentots and by the Dutch settlers at the Cape in the form of a pickle. They thrive best in sandy loam mixed with old lime and brick rubbish.

60. *Aloe africana* is so common that a description is scarcely needed, but we shall give some interesting particulars of the plant. The dark green leaves are numerous, and proceed from the outer part of the root; they are narrow, tapering, thick and fleshy, smooth, shining, and beset on the edges with spiny teeth. The African aloe is found about fifty miles from Cape Town, a mountain tract which is completely covered with them, and the hills on the west side of Socatra exhibit them in similar profusion. The species and varieties (150) all have stems, but vary in height from a few inches to thirty feet, with permanent succulent leaves. The negroes of the West Coast of Africa make

cords and nets of the fibres of their leaves, and
even stockings are woven with it. Aloes are chiefly
valued for their medicinal properties. The juice of
the aloe was in ancient times used in embalming to
preserve dead bodies from putrefaction. In the

Fig. 38.—ALOE AFRICANA (*b* the Flower.)

East Indies it is employed as a varnish to prevent
the attacks of insects. A beautiful violet colour is
obtained from the leaves of the *Socotrina aloe.*

We must observe that our plant is very unlike the
drawing we have given; but our Aloe is only an infant,

and we know how different the child is with his flaxen hair to the bearded man in after years.

61. *Pachyphytum roseum* has solid almond-shaped leaves, which are dusted with white similar to No. 35.

62. *Opuntia brasiliensis.*—Our plant may be said to be a miniature Opuntia. The parent stem is scarcely two inches high, it has on its edges seven little elliptical joints about an inch long by three-quarters of an inch in width. On the top of the uppermost joint another small one appears. For neatness, and we may add self-sufficiency, there is not another plant to match it in the case. We have been informed that these plants grow large, even twenty feet high; we trust, however, that ours will be contented to remain a dwarf.

63. *Opuntia cylindrica cristata.*—Of all grotesque plants this is one of the strangest, and it will be difficult to convey an idea of its form. The nearest approach to it is the form of the crimson cockscomb, if it can be imagined to be bent almost in two; or like a half solid circle or moon crumpled up; or, again, it may be described as an oval mass of vegetation about an inch thick, the oval not perfect, but bent about in wavy form, like a frill, crested at top, and spotted with white, where very fine spines protrude like hair. It is also crested on the top with green soft spines, as in *O. cylindrica*, No. 9. This

plant is apt at times to push out cylindrical shoots, which should be broken off, or the form of this Opuntia will be injured.

64. *Mesembryanthemum tigrinum.*—There is considerable difficulty in describing this remarkable plant; it is termed *tigrinum*, for as two leaves open at the same time they resemble the mouth of a tiger, with the teeth or fangs on each side of the upper and lower jaw; the roof of the mouth and tongue is represented. It is also spotted on the outside. The leaves are of singular form, and our readers may smile when we say they are of the exact shape of the head of a skiff or Thames pleasure boat, the prow is perfect, and even the deck is seen, but the resemblance stops here. It produces a bright yellow flower in October. We read that some species of these curious plants are called Cats-jaws, and also Dog-chaps, and even Wolf-chap, Fox-chap, Weasel-chap, Mouse-chap, Hatchet-leaved, Heron-beaked, Blunt-tongue, Bulls-horn, Boat-shaped, Boat-leaved, Hedge-hog—verily these plants are exceedingly remarkable.

65. *Mamillaria Wildiana*, a pretty little egg-shaped plant about one and a half inch in height of the usual *Mamillaria* character, covered with small spines, but it has this peculiarity that these are hooked—that is the extreme points are turned or bent backwards. This is not the only plant with this peculiarity.

We have been favoured with several plates from 'Loudon's Encyclopædia of Plants," published by Messrs. Longman, and the following are a few cuts which are given in that work and have not yet been alluded to.

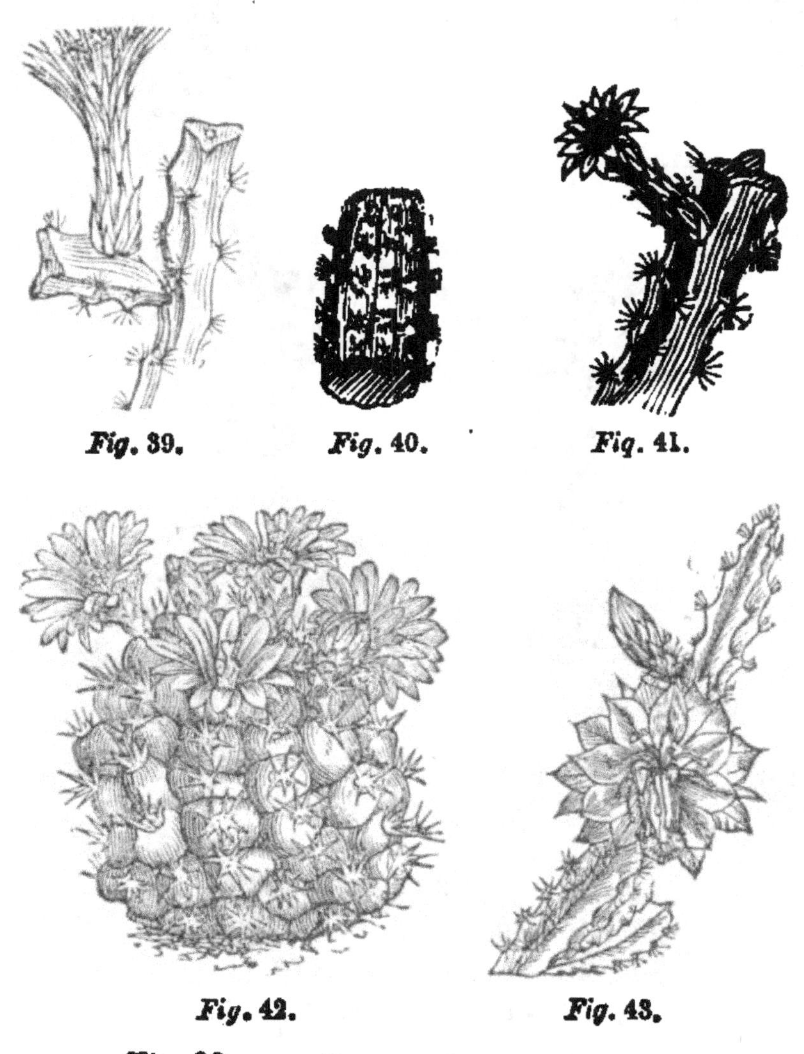

Fig. 39.   Fig. 40.   Fig. 41.

Fig. 42.   Fig. 43.

Fig. 39.—CEREUS TRIGONUS.
Fig. 40.—CEREUS LANUGINOSUS.
Fig. 41.—CEREUS QUADRANGULARIS.
Fig. 42.—ECHINOCACTUS MAMILLARIOIDES.
Fig. 43.—CEREUS SPECIOSISSIMUS.

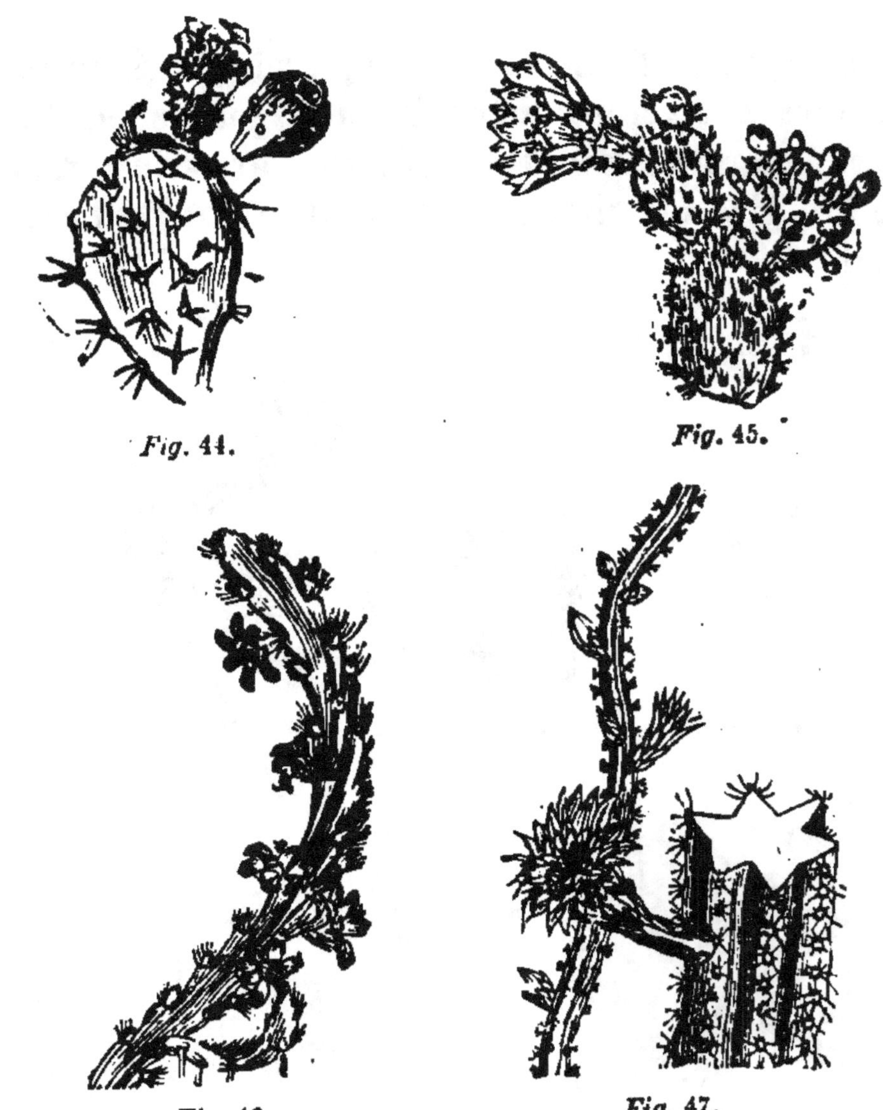

Fig. 44.   *Fig.* 45.

Fig. 46.   *Fig.* 47.

Fig. 44.—OPUNTIA NIGRICANS.
Fig. 45.—OPUNTIA POLYANTHA.
Fig. 46.—CEREUS SETOSUS.
Fig. 47.—CEREUS HEXAGONUS.

Loudon's Encyclopœdia of Plants, pages 110—12, gives a list of sixty-eight species of the Cactus, but these are now divided into several genera, viz., *Echinocactus, Echinopsis, Mamillaria, Cereus, Opuntia, &c.*

The following plants have been taken out of the Miniature Greenhouse to make room for others more suitable.

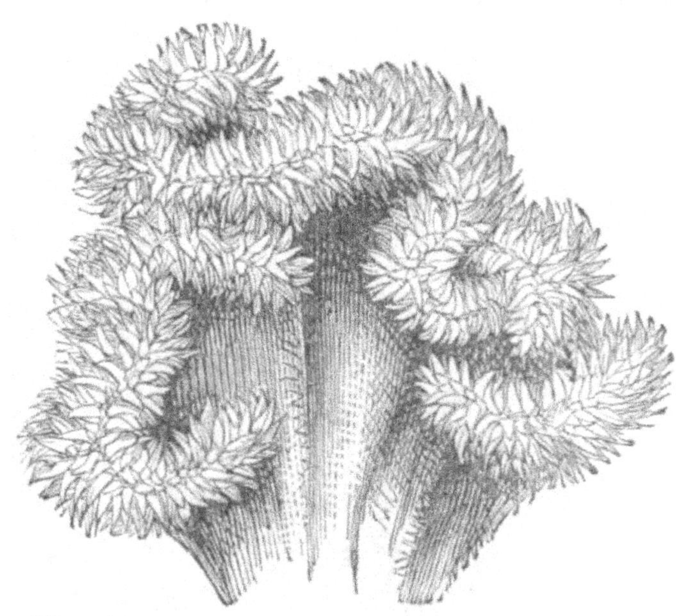

Fig. 48.—SEDUM REFLEXUM MONSTROSUM.

66. *Sedum reflexum monstrosum.*—A very curious plant, much like the cockscomb, but having a green irregular crest or fringe.   We have had two plants, but cannot keep them in our case, and if put out of doors the snails attack them as they do the *Aloe, Agave,* and *Echeveria metallica.*

67. *Mesembryanthemum linguæforme.*—This plant has light green fleshy leaves, very thick and formal. We had one, but from some cause or other it died. Flowers bright yellow.

68. *Sedum azoideum variegatum.*—A very pretty ornamental plant.   The foliage is light green, which

is beautifully marked with bands and margins of creamy white; it is of dwarf and bushy habit, and adorns a greenhouse when flowering plants have ceased to blow. A good bedding plant.

Fig. 49.—SEMPERVIVUM TABULÆFORME.

69. *Sempervivum tabulæforme* is a singular plant; it grows flat like a round table or plate, and is quite as large as the latter; is frequently used as a centre to a flower bed.

70. *Sedum Sieboldi* has trailing branches; the leaves, of glaucous hue, are highly ornamented with a wax-like blotch in the centre of each. This is an excellent plant for suspending in baskets. Flower rose colour.

71. *Mesembryanthemum conspicuum.*—The latter word signifies " clearly seen or excellent." This

plant is a very free grower, most suitable for rockeries; the light green leaves are long succulent spikes or spears; the flower is a bright red. A good plant for baskets. We fear we have killed it by over watering. [See remark at bottom of page 86.]

72. *Sedum ceruleum* is like the common stone crop, but of a bluish colour; very pretty for a bank or rockery; requires a poor sandy soil; we find it will not stand the frost out of doors.

Fig. 50.—SEMPERVIVUM CALCAREUM.

73. *Sempervivum calcareum* another plant of the House-leek family; also like No. 75, but the leaves are a fine green, with dark brown points; it is hardy; some gardeners call it *Californicum,* giving one the idea that it came from California, which is an error. It is worthy of remark that the rosette of the House-leek family is a scaly bulb of a lily, as it were, spread open, and produced on the surface of the ground instead of in the soil.

74. *Mesembryanthemum caulescens.*—A very pretty shrubby plant. The branches are covered with triangular solid bluish pods. Much recommended.

Fig. 51.—ECHEVERIA SECUNDA GLAUCA.

75. *Echeveria secunda glauca* is well known as a most useful bedding plant; generally employed as an edging; it is of the character of the House-leek, but of a silvery grayish white; it is very dwarf, and is frequently planted on its side, towards the outside of a flower-bed; they then have the appearance of a chain of rosettes. The young plants are thrown out at the sides like the House-leek, and they are also propagated by the leaves, which are put into a box of sandy soil, as thick as they can stand, and each soon displays a little bud at its base, which when more developed is potted into small pots; these when exposed to the light and in a brisk heat soon become healthy plants. Flower red and yellow.

76. *Saxifraga ceratophylla* grows in clusters, like London pride, but the individual plants are very small, only about the size of a sixpence; the edges of the leaves are serrated. The word *saxifraga* signifies stone breakers, as the roots of this family of plants are said to penetrate into rocks, and eventually break them. It has a white flower.

Fig. 52.—SEMPERVIVUM HIRTUM.

77. *Sempervivum hirtum* is sometimes called the family plant, as the mother plant is in the centre, and her little ones are grouped round as regular as if they were planted there by hand.

78. *Kleinia repens*—a peculiar plant, with long succulent pointed leaves; of a grayish-blue colour; it is said to have more blue in its foliage than any other plant, and is on this account useful for bedding.

79. *Saxifraga sarmentosa*—commonly known as mother of thousands; it will not stand frost; the leaves are prettily mottled and hairy; it propagates itself by runners like the strawberry; the young plants are seen at the end of the tendrils, and take root as soon as they find any soil. This plant is especially suitable to suspend in baskets.

80. *Crassula ericoides*—a prettily-formed plant; the narrow pointed leaves stand out at right angles with each other on its stem.

Fig. 53.—SEMPERVIVUM ARBOREUM.

81. *Sempervivum arboreum*—as No. 23, our plant has unfortunately died.

82. *Tradescantia zebrina*—a trailing green-house plant, of beautiful foliage; the light-green leaves have a shining glistening appearance, as though frosted, and are prettily marked down the middle with a shade of dark green; the under part of the leaf is pink. It is named from John Tradescant, gardener of Charles the First; this is not a succulent.

83. *Sedum carneum variegatum*—long spike-like leaves, striped with white and green.

Fig. 54.—ECHEVERIA METALLICA.

84. *Echeveria metallica*—one of the finest of ornamental foliaged plants; the leaves are large and massive, of metallic pinkish hue, like the brilliant necks of some pigeons. It is frequently used for the centre of a flower-bed. Flower yellow and rose.

85. *Saxifraga longifolia* is a pretty, dwarf, hardy plant of the character of No. 76, and rather similar to *Sempervivum calcareum*, No. 73, but the leaves are more narrow and pointed.

Fig. 55.—SEMPERVIVUM HAWORTHII.

86. *Sempervivum Haworthii* is a most curious plant, and may justly be called the miniature Banyan Tree ; its branches throw out fibres, which fall down and become additional roots to the plant.   We give this drawing from Mr. Cannel's "Floral Guide" (Swanley Junction Nurseries, Kent), to whom we are indebted for several wood-cuts.   We think that the downward roots are too large ; they should be drawn almost like threads.

87. *Sedum pulchellum*—similar to the common stone crop, but the leaves are a blood red ; these, however, turn green during the winter.

88. *Sedum dasyphyllum*—similar to the preceding, but of a white tint, and flower white.

CONCLUDING REMARKS.

After the description we have endeavoured to give of the plants that we possess, we think our readers will admit that succulents are very interesting and wonderful in their form. We have heard it remarked that anyone having but a small collection of such plants will care but little for geraniums and fuchsias, which after all are only pretty when in bloom. The blossoms of most of the Cacti are exceedingly beautiful, but whether they flower or not they are always remarkable productions of Nature. The very fact of their being denizens of various foreign lands adds to the interest with which we look on them. A correspondent in the *Gardener's Magazine*, under the name of "Wanderer," corroborates what we have written, in the following words:—"Of distinctive and striking form there is no end in this strange family of plants, but there is much of beauty too, and wondrous splendour. Nor are these the only qualities which entitle them to admiration. One of the fascinations attending the collecting and cultivating such plants, arises out of their longevity and individuality. The man who regards them in the right spirit is affected by their far removal from vegetable forms of fugacious habit, and ephemeral interest. They are not here to-day and gone to-morrow. You must get used to them; you must carefully study their habits and requirements; you must see them often, give them just the attention they require, abstain from merely meddling with them, and bring them to a certain extent into your inmost being, so that when far away you will think of your gaunt, weird, and it may be gigantic pets at home, and find in the intellectual macrocosm proof that you did wisely to select these for special study and cultivation."

During the cold weather in the winter the temperature in our room did not fall below 40°, and at such times we covered the case with a large railway wrapper; if the thermometer had indicated a lower temperature we must have had a small lamp in the case, or a fire in the room.

Out of so many plants it would be unreasonable to suppose that we could save all through the winter; we lost six or seven out of about 54, they gradually withered and died, whether from want of heat, or too much or too little water, we are unable to say. With the generality of succulents, we are more likely to err by giving them too much water than too little. Once in about three weeks or a month is quite enough during the winter, while in their dormant state, and it is asserted that they like to be pot-bound.

It is well, perhaps, not to be too successful in anything, and it enhances the value of those plants we are enabled to preserve when we lose others; indeed, if a few die it affords us an opportunity of having different plants in their places, and our experience consequently becomes more extended.

We cannot but feel a little anxiety on one point; slowly as they grow there will come a time when some of our plants get beyond bounds; we certainly have no accommodation for any of our pets if they get too tall and bulky. We suppose our only course will then be to exchange such for smaller plants.

We have quite lately found that Miss Maling, in her work on "Indoor Plants," speaks of a small glass case three feet long by eighteen inches wide and high, which she had constructed with a heating apparatus at the cost of two guineas. The case was lined with zinc, but without a boiler, for she adopts a zinc hot water case or pan two inches deep, which fits loosely into the outer trough or box of six inches in depth, which contains silver sand for forcing the plants. The boiler or zinc hot water case is filled from a pipe passing through the wood-work at one end, and there is a small brass cock for drawing the water off. A very small pipe inside, about two inches long, provides for the due escape of the air, without which, of course, the case could not be filled or emptied. When the escape of steam is too great, a cork may be put into this pipe, but the cork must be withdrawn before the re-filling commences. When the case is not required for forcing, it is in itself a small conservatory. The ends, sides, and top of the case are each formed of one large pane of glass, the top and one side being separately framed so as to take in and out in order

to give greater facility both for cleaning and
arranging the plants within.   The glass top should
be so made that it can be opened about one or two
inches, or the entire front panel may be often kept
out all day.   The woodwork should be very light; it
can be made of any wood or painted of any colour,
but veneered wood will not do, as the damp injures
it.   In spring, which is the principal time when
artificial heat is needed, the zinc case being filled
with boiling water night and morning, the heat
varies from 55° to 75°; indeed, it could easily be had
at 90°, especially when the silver sand is a little
moist and the soil in the pots effectually retains
the heat, often feeling quite warm even four
and twenty hours after the boiler has been
filled.   A woollen cover to place over the case on
any particularly cold night is very useful to stop the
escape of heat, and prevent the great condensation
of steam upon the glass.   As the dripping of any
moisture is very injurious to the plants it falls on, a
slope of four inches in the roof, and a gutter along
the front to catch and carry down the water, might
be an improvement.   Cases that require a lamp or
a jet of gas to be kept almost continually burning
underneath the boiler Miss Maling does not recommend.   If the expense of two guineas is objected to
she remarks that any tea or orange box could
be cut down and used for the purpose, but it must
be fitted with a zinc pan for hot water; in this
instance a large pane of glass resting on the top

would answer the purpose. A sponge is useful to remove any moisture that collects on the glass.

Our readers may desire to know where Cacti can be obtained. We have procured them here and there as opportunities arose; some we purchased in Covent Garden and from other florists in minute thumb pots, at 6*d.* each, but of course we put them into large pots immediately; it is a pity they are sold in pots so small, for there is little chance of their living. In taking our walks we frequently meet with good plants at some out-of-the-way nursery; thus when out one day we obtained an excellent plant of (No. 10 in our list) *Mesembryanthemum densum,* and (No. 6) *Crassula lycopodioides,* for only threepence each—most of our plants cost sixpence; perhaps others would prefer larger plants at 2*s.* or 3*s.*—and some have been kindly given to us or exchanged for duplicates which we possessed. We cannot advertise a man's business, but if inquiry be made there will be no particular difficulty in collecting together a pretty little stock, and after a while you can do as we have done, turn out the commoner plants to make room for others more interesting; the generality of florists do not keep Cacti. Mr. Croucher, of Brook Green, Hammersmith, is a well-known authority, from whose writings on the subject we have given some extracts. We believe he would kindly afford information as to where particular plants can be obtained, but persons writing to him should not forget to enclose a stamped envelope for a reply. You can go to almost any expense, but it is useless to get delicate valuable plants if you have no proper mode of keeping them; we could have far more beautiful Cacti, &c., than we possess if we

Fig. 56.—PILOCEREUS SENILIS (OLD MAN CACTUS).

Drawn by Mr. Rogers, 200, Fleet-street, from a plant in Mr. Peacock's collection.

had a place that could be heated in the winter. We are obliged to content ourselves with what are comparatively hardy and common; some of the plants of the Old Man Cactus are about two guineas each, and doubtless Mr. Peacock's collection at Hammer-smith (to which we have alluded in the preface) is worth several thousand pounds. Only imagine the great age of some of the plants; no wonder therefore that they should be so valuable.

The Royal Gardens at Kew* are open daily, and can be seen free of charge. Mr. Peacock's collection of succulents, we believe, can also be visited on application by letter to Sudbury House, Hammersmith. Amongst these extensive collections we particularly noticed the *Pilocereus Dautwitzi*, which is about eight inches high, with its spines covered with long wool—not standing out like hair, as in the *Old Man cactus*, but spun round the plant; the *Mamillaria sphærotricha* also appears as though wrapped round with white silk. Then, again, if we turn to the *Cacti*, we see that some of their ribs or angles, instead of being perpendicular, run diagonally round the cactus in spiral lines. Some of the *Gasteria* also have a spiral twist. Then we observe a few of the *Mamillaria* have what appears to be little white tufts of cotton-wadding between the protuberances; this is specially the case with the *Mamillaria cirrhifera megacantha* and *rufispina*. Next, that the spines of the *Cacti* are of divers colours—some black, some red, and others yellow and white. A drawing of a tuft of spines is given in the following page; but these clusters differ in the number and shape of the spines in various *Cacti*, &c.

---

* The Gardeners' Chronicle published a supplement in August last giving an admirably written description of the Royal Gardens at Kew, embellished with several views of the conservatories, &c.

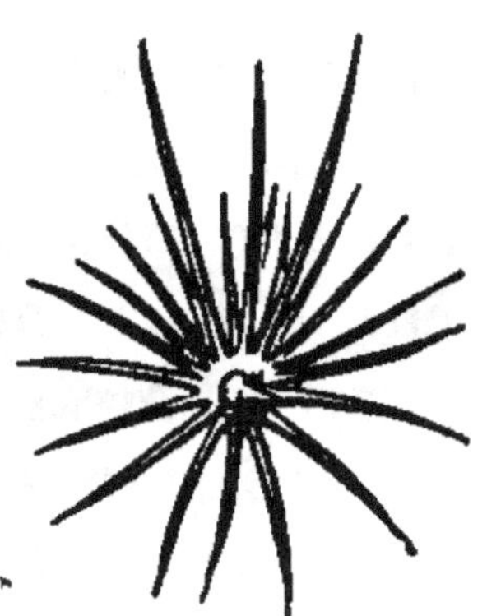

Fig. 57.—CLUSTER OF SPINES FROM THE ECHINOCACTUS
INTERTEXTUS.

The *Cereus peruvianus monstrosus* is a most grotesque-growing plant; it resembles a mass of green vitrified pottery run together in an irregular form. To turn to smaller plants: how singular is the *Crassula perfoliata,* with its leaves threaded on the stalk; it actually runs through the middle of the leaves. Could anything be more pure and delicate than the *Kleinia Haworthii* or *tomentosa,* with its spear-shaped slender leaves, its downish-white exterior like frosted silver, soft and silken to the touch. Amongst the collection of *Agaves* we see how gracefully their massive fleshy leaves curve downwards after a certain elevation. Contrast these noble plants with the totally different form of the *Agave hystrix,* which has long pointed spikes or spears all jutting or standing out from its centre; these, radiating all round top and sides alike, seem to bid defiance to any one to reach its heart. The *Agave Richardsii* also is of this form. Then, again, consider what we have read in this work, that some plants are of such extreme delicacy that their flowers cannot bear the action of full light, but open their beauteous blossoms only at night (p. 22). Time would fail us to speak more on this subject; but surely these succulents deserve a larger share of attention than most people are content to bestow on them.

In conclusion, we would observe that one special advantage in the plan we have described is that we can always have the pleasure of seeing our plants without the trouble of going outside the house; there is no need to go through the rain or to a conservatory in the garden, if we wish to spend a half hour with our " second family." We frequently have a look at some of them before retiring for the night, and many a summer's morning we have been engaged for an hour or so examining the state of this or that plant, long before any one else stirred in the house. Unless there is an entrance into a conservatory from the house, you cannot go there of an evening after dark on returning from business, but our Miniature Greenhouse is always ready at hand to interest us.

We close our remarks with the Gardener's motto from Mr. Cannell's " Floral Guide ":—

> " Work on, hope on ; and be ye sure
> Self-help is noble schooling ;
> You do your best, and leave the rest
> To God Almighty's ruling."

Price 6½d., or half-bound, with writing-paper for memoranda, 1s. 8d. by post

A SYSTEM FOR CROPPING A KITCHEN GARDEN:

A Rotation clearly explained, for the use of Amateur Gardeners.

By HENRY ALLNUTT.

"We can safely say, that by following the directions herein given, the reader may possess himself of all that is promised."—*Gardeners' Chronicle.*

Also, by the same Author, price 1s. 2d. or half-bound, in cloth, 1s. 8d. by post.

OUR FLOWER GARDEN:

HOW WE MADE THE MOST OF IT.

With instructions as to building Miniature Ruins for Fern Cases. Second Edition, much enlarged.

Also, by the same Author,

WHEAT DIAGRAMS.

Diagram showing the Rise and Fall in the Price of Wheat annually, from 1641 to the present time, 1s. 1d., free by post; mounted on rollers and varnished, 5s. Also, Diagrams of the Price of Wheat weekly, from 1858 to the present time, 3d. each year.

These Diagrams can be had bound in a book, space being allowed for the insertion of future years, 5s.

"ESTATES GAZETTE" OFFICE, 200, FLEET STREET, LONDON.

Also, by the same Author,

THE HISTORICAL DIARY OF THE FRANCO-GERMAN WAR;

Being a Compilation of the most important and deeply interesting events that have appeared in the public press. This work abounds in thrilling incidents. It includes a small Map of Paris, showing the Fortifications, German Batteries, and their Range, &c. 416 pages, best cloth, reduced from 5s. 4d. to 3s. 4d., in boards from 4s. 4d. to 2s. 4d., by post.

DIARY OF EVENTS, from the above; being a brief outline of the Franco-German War. 4d.

Also, by the same Author,

RECORD MAP OF THE FRANCO-GERMAN WAR,

Extending east to west from Berlin to Le Mans, and north to south from the Baltic to Switzerland; showing, by red flags, the situation of 22 Battles, and, by red disks, the occupation of upwards of 60 French towns. One large sheet, 4 × 4½ft., coloured; scale about 12 miles to an inch. Mounted to fold in case, or on rollers, varnished; with Map of Paris and Abstract of Events, arranged chronologically, reduced from 15s. 6d. to 10s. 6d. by post.

SMALL EDITION of the above MAP of the WAR, same scale, but only that portion where the War actually occurred, extending from the Rhine to Le Mans, and not including Berlin and the Baltic; coloured, in sheet, 34 × 21 inches, reduced from 2s. 6d. to 1s. 1d. by post; mounted, to fold in case, or on rollers, varnished, reduced from 6s. to 3s. 3d. by post.

"ESTATES GAZETTE" OFFICE, 200, FLEET STREET, LONDON.

www.ingramcontent.com/pod-product-compliance
Lightning Source LLC
Chambersburg PA
CBHW081615250726
48657CB00009B/2584